Coats & Clark

QUILTING *for beginners*

CREATIVE
PUBLISHING
international

Contents

Introduction . . . . .Page 4

The Sewing Machine . . . . .Page 6

Machine Accessories . . . . .Page 8

Getting Ready to Sew . . . . .Page 10

How to Balance Tension .Page 14

Quilt Seams . . . . .Page 16

Quilting Supplies . . . . .Page 18

Fabric Information . . . . .Page 23

Selecting the Batting . . . . .Page 29

Rotary Cutting . . . . .Page 30

Layering & Basting . . . . .Page 34

Basic Quilting Techniques . . . . .Page 38

Binding . . . . .Page 42

Raw-edge Appliqué Hot Pad . . . . . . .Page 47

Nine-patch Pillow . . . . .Page 53

Checkerboard Placemats . . . . . .Page 61

Double Nine-patch Table Topper . .Page 69

Pieced Sashing Table Runner . . . .Page 77

Log Cabin Sewing Machine Cover . . . . .Page 85

Bow Ties Wall Hanging . . . . .Page 93

Ohio Star Flange Pillow . . . . .Page 103

Flannel Lap Quilt . . . . .Page 113

Rail Fence Wall Hanging .Page 119

Glossary . . . . .Page 124

Index . . . . .Page 126

QUILTING FOR BEGINNERS

Created by:
The Editors of Creative Publishing international, Inc.

Library of Congress Cataloging-in-Publication Data
Quilting for beginners.
    p. cm. -- (Seams sew easy)
  Includes index.
  ISBN 0-86573-327-9 (HC)
  1. Patchwork--Patterns. 2. Quilting--Patterns. 3. Quilted goods.
I. Creative Publishing international. II. Series.
TT835.Q47 1998
746.46'041--dc21   98-28530

How to *Use This Book*

Welcome to the rewarding world of sewing. The *Seams Sew Easy*™ series of books is designed to encourage creativity and instill confidence as you learn to sew. Easy-to-follow instructions with colorful photographs and illustrations help you build your sewing skills while making home decorating and apparel items that are as useful as they are appealing.

Quilting, once a necessary household activity, is now considered an art form. The color combinations and patterns are limited only by your imagination. Many quilters prefer traditional quilt patterns, but quilts also can be designed in a modern, bold, or whimsical style to complement any decor. If you're learning to sew, quilting is a great way to hone your skills of cutting, piecing, pressing, and stitching with accuracy. And there's no need to purchase expensive fabrics; you may find a purpose for even the smallest pieces of leftover material.

This book will teach you, step-by-step, how to make great-looking quilted projects while you're learning the fundamentals of sewing. The ten quilting projects provide a sampling of a range of quilt block patterns. With each project you'll learn new skills, listed under WHAT YOU'LL LEARN. You will also find tips and explanations throughout the book to help you understand the "why" behind the instructions. And while the projects suggest size and color combinations, the possibilities are endless. Try the variations found at the end of the projects, or experiment with your own design and fabric choices.

Use the first section of the book to acquaint yourself with the sewing machine and the techniques and supplies you'll need to get started. Your sewing machine owner's manual is a necessity; refer to it first if you have questions or problems specific to your machine.

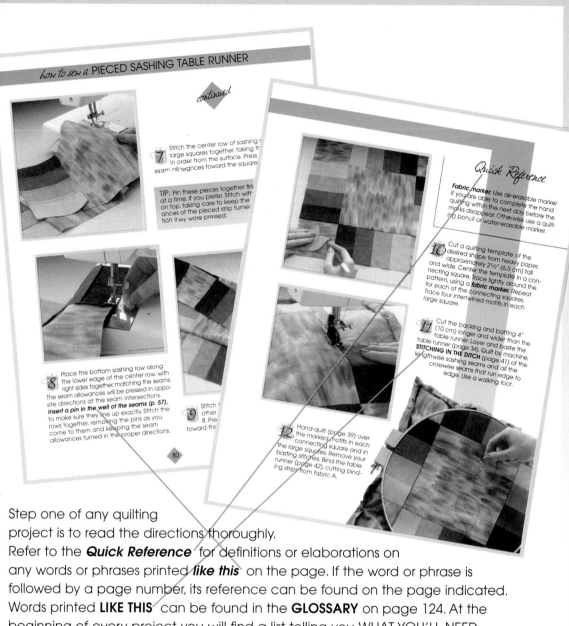

continued

7 Stitch the center row of sashing s...
large squares together, taking th...
in order from the surface. Press
seam allowances toward the square...

TIP: Pin these pieces together firs...
at a time, if you prefer. Stitch wit...
on top, taking care to keep the
ances of the pieced strip turne...
tion they were pressed.

8 Place the bottom sashing row along
the lower edge of the center row, with
right sides together, matching the seams.
The seam allowances will be pressed in opposite directions at the seam intersections.
Insert a pin in the well of the seams (p. 57),
to make sure they line up exactly. Stitch the
rows together, removing the pins as you
come to them and keeping the seam
allowances turned in the proper directions.

80

9 Stitch '...
other...
8. Pre...
toward the...

Quick Reference

Fabric marker. Use air-erasable marker
if you are able to complete the hand
quilting within the next day before the
marks disappear. Otherwise use a quilting pencil or water-erasable marker.

10 Cut a quilting template of the
desired shape from heavy paper,
approximately 2½" (6.5 cm) tall
and wide. Center the template in a connecting square. Trace lightly around the
pattern, using a *fabric marker.* Repeat
for each of the connecting squares.
Trace four intertwined motifs in each
large square.

11 Cut the backing and batting 4"
(10 cm) longer and wider than the
table runner. Layer and baste the
table runner (page 34). Quilt by machine,
STITCHING IN THE DITCH (page 41) of the
lengthwise sashing seams and all the
crosswise seams that run edge to
edge. Use a walking foot.

12 Hand-quilt (page 39) over
the marked motifs in each
connecting square and in
the large squares. Remove your
basting stitches. Bind the table
runner (page 42), cutting binding strips from fabric A.

Step one of any quilting
project is to read the directions thoroughly.
Refer to the **Quick Reference** for definitions or elaborations on
any words or phrases printed *like this* on the page. If the word or phrase is
followed by a page number, its reference can be found on the page indicated.
Words printed **LIKE THIS** can be found in the **GLOSSARY** on page 124. At the
beginning of every project you will find a list telling you WHAT YOU'LL NEED.
Read through the information on fabrics before you go shopping, so the fabric
store will seem a little more user-friendly when you get there.

Most of all, have fun! These quilting projects are a great opportunity for
creativity and expression of your personal style.

The Sewing Machine

The principle parts common to all modern sewing machines are shown in the diagrams at right. The parts may look different on your model, and they may have slightly different locations, so open your owner's manual, also. If you do not have an owner's manual for your machine, you should be able to get one from a sewing machine dealer who sells your brand. Become familiar with the names of the parts and their functions. As you spend more time sewing, these items will become second nature to you.

If you are buying a new machine, consider how much and what kind of sewing you expect to do. Talk to friends who sew and to sales personnel. Ask for demonstrations, and sew on the machine yourself. Experiment with the various features while sewing on a variety of fabrics, including knits, wovens, lightweights, and denim. Think about the optional features of the machine and which ones you want on yours. Many dealers offer free sewing lessons with the purchase of a machine. Take advantage! These lessons will be geared to your particular brand and model of sewing machine.

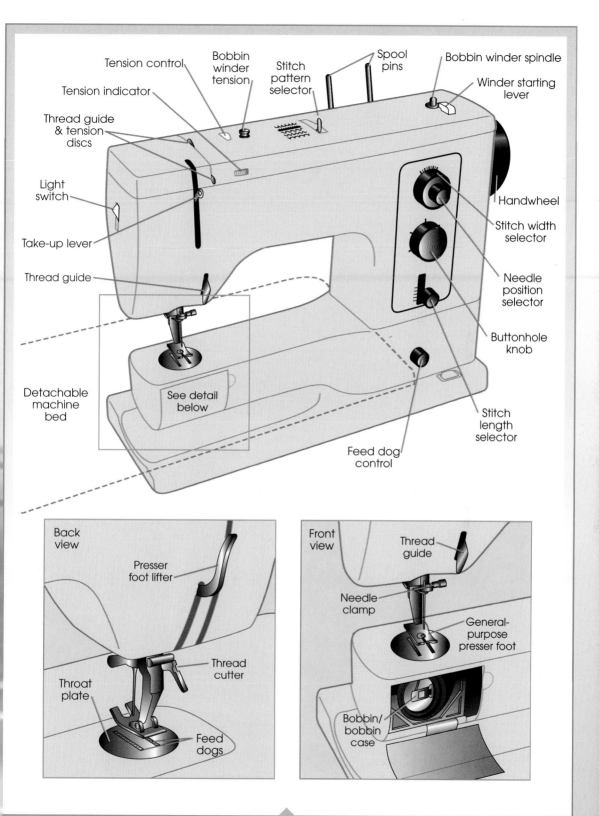

Tension control

Bobbin winder tension

Stitch pattern selector

Spool pins

Bobbin winder spindle

Tension indicator

Winder starting lever

Thread guide & tension discs

Light switch

Handwheel

Stitch width selector

Take-up lever

Needle position selector

Thread guide

Buttonhole knob

Detachable machine bed

See detail below

Stitch length selector

Feed dog control

Back view

Presser foot lifter

Thread cutter

Throat plate

Feed dogs

Front view

Thread guide

Needle clamp

General-purpose presser foot

Bobbin/bobbin case

Machine *Accessories*

Sewing Machine Needles

Sewing machine needles come in a variety of styles and sizes. The correct needle choice depends mostly on the fabric you have selected. Sharp points **(A)**, used for woven fabrics, are designed to pierce the fabric. Ballpoints **(B)** are designed to slip between the loops of knit fabric rather than pierce and possibly damage the fabric. Universal points **(C)** are designed to work on both woven and knitted fabrics. The size of the needle is designated by a number, generally given in both European (60, 70, 80, 90, 100, 110) and American (9, 11, 12, 14, 16, 18) numbering systems. Use size 11/70 or 12/80 needles for any of the fabrics you would find suitable for your quilted projects. A larger number means the needle is thicker and that it is appropriate for use with heavier fabrics and heavier threads.

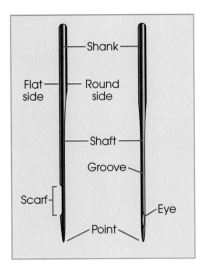

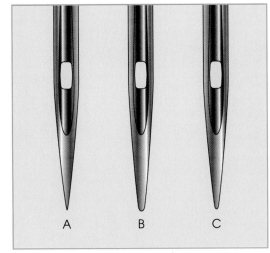

TIP: Though needle style and size are usually indicated in some way on the needle, it is often difficult to see without a magnifying glass, and you most likely will not remember what needle is in the machine. As an easy reminder, when you finish a sewing session, leave a fabric swatch from your current project under the presser foot.

Bobbins

Stitches are made by locking the upper thread with a lower thread, carried on a bobbin. Always use bobbins in the correct style and size for your machine. Bobbin thread tension is controlled by a spring on the bobbin case, which may be built in **(A)** or removable **(B)**.

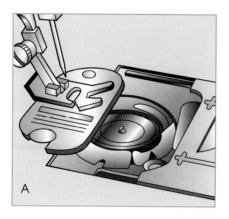

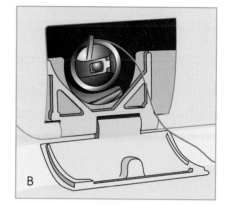

Presser Feet

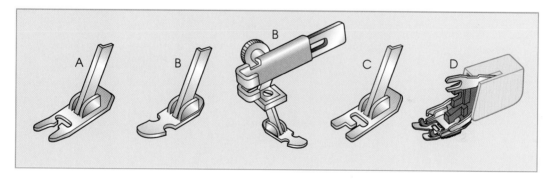

Every sewing machine comes with accessories for specialized tasks. More can be purchased as you develop your interest and skills. Your machine manual or dealer can show you what accessories are available and will explain how to use them to get the best results.

A general-purpose foot **(A),** probably the one you will use most often, has a wide opening to accommodate the side-to-side movement of the needle in all types of utility (nondecorative) stitches. It is also suitable for most straight stitching. A zipper foot **(B)** is used to insert zippers or to stitch any

seam that has more bulk on one side than the other. For some sewing machines, the zipper foot is stationary, requiring you to move the needle position to the right or left. For other styles, the position of the zipper foot itself is adjustable. A special-purpose or embroidery foot **(C)** has a grooved bottom that allows the foot to ride smoothly over decorative stitches or raised cords. Some styles are clear plastic, allowing you to see your work more clearly. A walking foot **(D)** feeds top and bottom layers at equal rates, allowing you to more easily match patterns or stitch bulky layers, as in quilted projects.

Getting *Ready to Sew*

Simple tasks of inserting the needle, winding the bobbin, and threading the machine have tremendous influence on the stitch quality and performance of your machine. Use this guide as a general reference, but refer to your owner's manual for instructions specific to your machine.

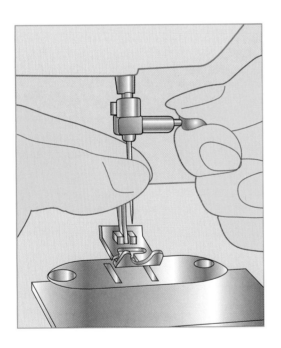 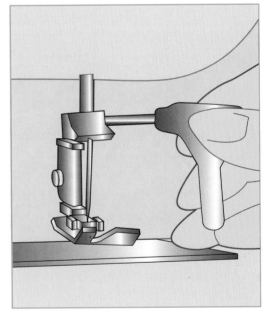

Inserting the Needle

Loosen the needle clamp. After selecting the appropriate needle for your project (page 8), insert it into the machine as high as it will go. The grooved side of the needle faces forward, if your bobbin gets inserted from the front or top; it faces to the left, if your bobbin gets inserted on the left. Tighten the clamp securely.

Winding the Bobbin

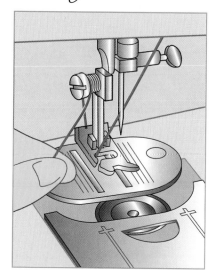

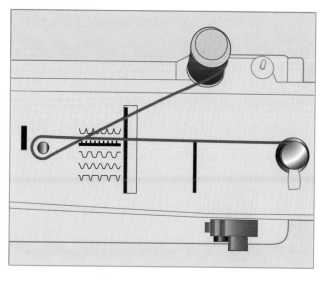

If the bobbin case is built in, the bobbin is wound in place with the machine fully threaded as if to sew (page 12).

Removable bobbins are wound on the top or side of the machine, with the machine threaded for bobbin winding, as described in your owner's manual.

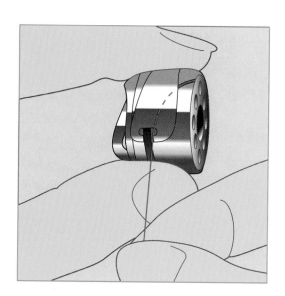

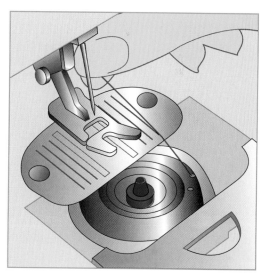

Bobbin thread must be drawn through the bobbin case tension spring. For wind-in-place bobbins, this happens automatically when you wind the bobbin, but you must do it manually when you insert a bobbin that already has thread on it.

continued

Threading the Machine

Because every sewing machine is different, the threading procedure for your machine may differ slightly from the one shown here. Once again, it is important to refer to your owner's manual. Every upper thread guide adds a little tension to the thread as it winds its way to the needle. Missing one of them can make a big difference in the quality of your stitches.

 Set the thread spool on the spindle.

A. Vertical spindle. Position the spool so that it will turn clockwise as you sew.

B. Horizontal spindle. The spool is held in place with an end cap. If your spool has a small cut in one end for minding the thread, position the spool with that end to the right.

TIP: If the spool is new and has paper labels covering the holes, poke them in, completely uncovering the holes, to allow the spool to turn freely.

Unless your machine has a self-winding bobbin, you will want to wind the bobbin before threading the machine (page 11).

 Pull thread to the left and through the first thread guide.

 Draw thread through the tension guide.

TIP: It is very important to have the presser foot lever up when threading the machine, because the tension discs are then open. If the presser foot is down and the discs are closed, the thread will not slide between the discs, and your stitches will not make you happy.

 Draw thread through the next thread guide.

 Insert thread through the take-up lever.

 Draw the thread through the remaining thread guides.

 Thread the needle. Most needles are threaded from front to back; some, from left to right.

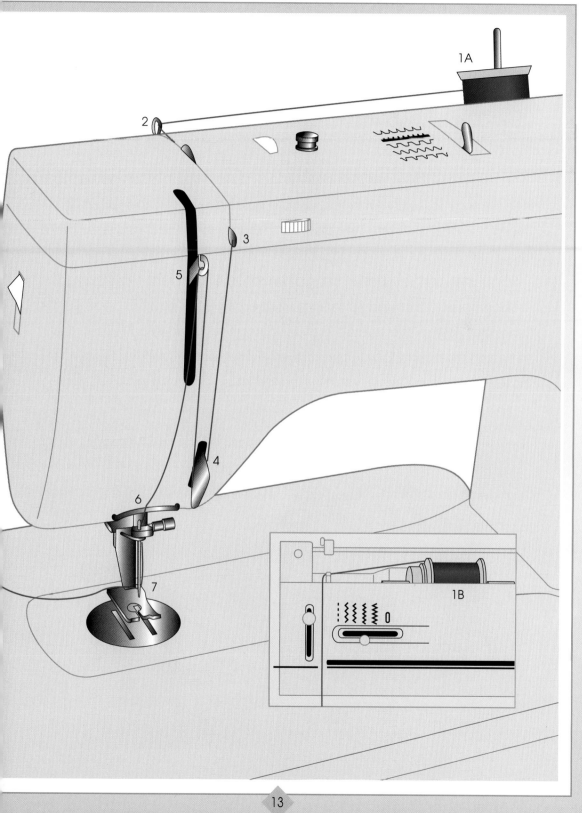

How to Balance Tension

Your machine forms stitches by interlocking the bobbin thread with the needle thread. Every time the needle goes down into the fabric, a sharp hook catches the needle thread and wraps the bobbin thread around it. Imagine this little tug-of-war. If the needle thread tension is "stronger" than the bobbin thread tension, the needle thread pulls the bobbin thread through to the top. If the bobbin thread tension is "stronger," it pulls the needle thread through to the bottom. When the tensions are evenly balanced, the stitch will lock exactly halfway between the top and bottom of the layers being sewn, which is right where you want it.

Some machines have "self-adjusting tension," meaning the machine automatically adjusts its tension with every fabric you sew. For machines that do not have this feature, you may have to adjust the needle thread tension slightly as you sew different fabrics.

Testing the Tension

1. Thread your machine and insert the bobbin, using two very different colors of thread, neither of which matches the fabric. Cut an 8" (20.5 cm) square of a smooth, mediumweight fabric. Fold the fabric in half diagonally, and place it under the presser foot so the fold aligns to your 1/2" (1.3 cm) seam guide. Lower the presser foot and set your stitch length at 10 stitches per inch or 2.5 mm long.

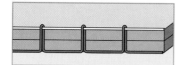 Stitch a line across the fabric, stitching ½" (1.3 cm) from the diagonal fold. Remove the fabric from the machine. Inspect your stitching line from both sides. If your tension is evenly balanced, you will see only one color on each side. If you see both thread colors on the top side of your sample, the needle tension is tighter than the bobbin tension. If you see both thread colors on the back side of your sample, the bobbin tension is tighter than the needle tension.

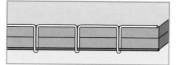

Top tension too tight

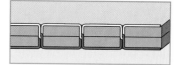

Top tension too loose

Tensions even

Adjusting the Tension

Before adjusting the tension on your machine, first check:
- that your machine is properly threaded (page 12)
- that your bobbin is properly installed
- that your needle is not damaged and is inserted correctly

 Pull on your stitching line until you hear threads break. (Because you stitched on the **BIAS**, the fabric will stretch slightly.) If the thread breaks on only one side, your machine's tension is tighter on that side.

After checking these three things, you may need to adjust the tension on your machine. (Check your owner's manual.) Tighten or loosen the needle thread tension *slightly* to bring the needle thread and bobbin thread tensions into balance. Test the stitches after each adjustment, until you achieve balanced tension. If slight adjustments of the needle tension dial do not solve the problem, the bobbin tension may need adjusting. However, most manufacturers do not recommend that you adjust bobbin tension yourself, so unless you have received instructions for your machine, take your machine to the repairman.

Quilt *Seams*

Quilting is like putting puzzles together. Lots of squares, rectangles, triangles, and fabric strips are pieced together to make a colorful fabric picture. Every **SEAM** is sewn using 1/4" (6 mm) **SEAM ALLOWANCES.** In order to make all the pieces fit precisely, you must sew every seam accurately. Most machines have a seam allowance guide on the throat plate; however, it may not include a mark for 1/4" (6 mm). Often, the distance from the needle tip to the edge of the presser foot is exactly 1/4" (6 mm). If neither of these guides works for your machine, mark a 1/4" (6 mm) seam guide on the bed of your machine with tape.

Making a Seam Guide

Mark a line 1/4" (6 mm) from the edge on a small square of fabric. Put the fabric under the presser foot, so that the marked line aligns to the tip of the needle. Place tape on the bed of the machine even with the cut edge of the fabric. Use the tape as a guide for sewing all your seams.

Sewing Seams

1. Thread your machine (page 12) and insert the bobbin (page 11). Holding the needle thread with your left hand, turn the handwheel toward you until the needle has gone down and come back up to its highest point. A stitch will form, and you will feel a tug on the needle thread. Pull on the needle thread to bring the bobbin thread up through the hole in the throat plate. Pull both threads together under the presser foot and off to one side.

2. Place two fabric squares right sides together, aligning the outer edges. Pin the pieces together along one long edge, inserting the pins perpendicular to the edge. Place the fabric under the presser foot so the pinned side edges align to the 1/4" (6 mm) seam guide and the upper edges align to the needle hole in the throat plate. Lower the presser foot, and set your stitch length at 2 mm, which equals 15 stitches per inch.

3 Begin stitching slowly. Hold the thread tails under a finger for the first few stitches. This prevents the needle thread from being pulled out of the needle and also prevents the thread tails from being drawn down into the bobbin case, where they could potentially cause the dreaded *thread jam.* Gently guide the fabric while you sew by walking your fingers ahead of and slightly to the sides of the presser foot. Remember, you are only guiding; let the machine pull the fabric.

Quick Reference

Thread jam. No matter how conscientious you are at trying to prevent them, thread jams just seem to be lurking out there waiting to mess up your day. DON'T USE FORCE! Remove the presser foot, if you can. Snip all the threads you can get at from the top of the throat plate. Open the bobbin case door or throat plate, and snip any threads you can get at. Remove the bobbin, if you can. Gently remove the fabric. Thoroughly clean out the feed dog and bobbin area before reinserting the bobbin and starting over. Then just chalk it up to experience and get over it!

> TIP: Straight stitching lines are easier to achieve if you watch the edge of the fabric along the seam guide and ignore the needle. Sew smoothly at a relaxing pace, with minimal starting and stopping, and without bursts of speed. You have better control of the speed if you operate your foot control with your heel resting on the floor.

4 Stop stitching and remove pins as you come to them. When you reach the end of the fabric, stop again. Turn the handwheel toward you until the needle is in its highest position.

5 Raise the presser foot. Pull the fabric smoothly away from the presser foot, either to the left side or straight back. If you have to tug the threads, turn your handwheel slightly toward you until they pull easily. Cut the threads, leaving tails on the fabric and coming from the machine.

Quilting

Supplies

The process of quilting involves several basic tasks: measuring, cutting, marking, and stitching. For each of these steps there are special tools and supplies to save you time, improve your accuracy, and make the project go smoothly.

Measuring & Cutting Tools

Buy quality cutting tools and use them only for sewing! Cutting paper and other non-fabric materials will dull your tools quickly. Sharp tools make precise cuts easier and, in the long run, will save you time.

Rotary cutters **(A)** allow you to cut smooth edges on multiple layers of fabric quickly

and easily. The cutters are available in different sizes. Small cutters work well for curves and a few layers of fabric; the larger ones are ideal for long straight lines and many layers of fabric.

Cutting mats **(B),** made especially for use with rotary cutters, protect your blade and

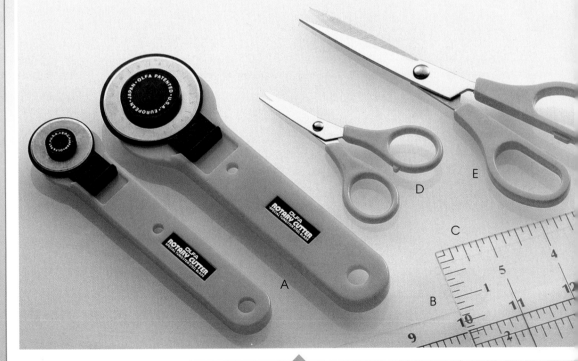

table top. Mats come in a variety of sizes. Choose one at least 22" (56 cm) wide to accommodate a width of fabric folded in half. A mat with a printed grid is a useful guide for cutting right angles.

You'll want a clear ruler **(C)** to use as a measuring tool and as a guide for your rotary cut-

ter. A ruler 6"x 24" (15 x 61 cm) is a popular, versatile size. Square rulers and rulers with 30°, 45°, and 60° angle lines also are available.

Sewing scissors **(D)** and shears **(E)** are sewing necessities. Purchase the best quality you can afford.

Marking Tools

The marks you make on fabric should last only as long as you need them. You should be able to remove them easily without damaging the quilt. Always test a marker on a sample swatch of fabric first and remember to mark lightly!

A special fabric eraser **(F)** can be used to remove light lead pencil marks without damaging fabric. Quilter's pencils **(G),** available

in white or gray lead, have eraser ends for easy removal. The leads are oil-free and contain less graphite to prevent smearing. Soapstone pencils **(H),** made of pressed talc, can be sharpened to a fine point and rubbed off or wiped with a damp cloth. Water-soluble pencils **(I),** handy for marking on darker fabrics, can be removed with a damp cloth.

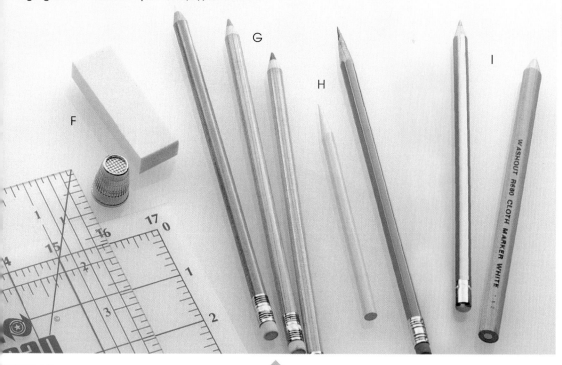

Pins, Needles & Thread

A Quilting pins, used for pinning your pieces together, are 1³/4" (4.5 cm) long and have large glass heads.

B Rustproof safety pins in 1" to 1¹/2" (2.5 to 3.8 cm) size make quick work of basting your quilting projects.

C Milliner's needles with small, round eyes are preferred by quilters who want to hand-baste the layers.

D Betweens are short needles with round eyes, for sewing small hand-quilting stitches.

E Cotton-covered polyester threads and 100% cotton threads are available for machine and hand quilting. Hand-quilting threads have a polished glacé finish that provides abrasion resistance and prevents tangling and knotting; 100% cotton basting thread is also available.

F Fine monofilament thread can also be used for machine quilting, making the stitches less noticeable.

Pressing at each stage of construction is the secret to perfect piecing. The general rule is to press each stitched seam before crossing it with another. Often you can sew the same seam in numerous sets before making the trip to the ironing board to press them all.

Pressing your seams carefully is crucial to your success, second only to accurate sewing of the 1/4" (6 mm) seams. Use the tip of the iron, moving only in the direction of the **GRAINLINES.** Be especially cautious when pressing seams sewn on the **BIAS.** Careless pressing can distort the shape and size of your quilt project. Both **SEAM ALLOWANCES** are usually pressed together to one side or the other. Following the pressing plan in the project directions will help you produce a neat, precise design.

Use a steam/spray iron with a wide temperature range. Buy a dependable, name-brand iron. Because your iron will be left on and standing still for several minutes between pressing steps, avoid an iron with an automatic shut-off feature.

An ironing board provides a sufficient surface for pressing, but you may want to invest in a fold-out surface, such as this Spaceboard™. It has a cotton cover printed with a measured grid to help you press your pieces more accurately.

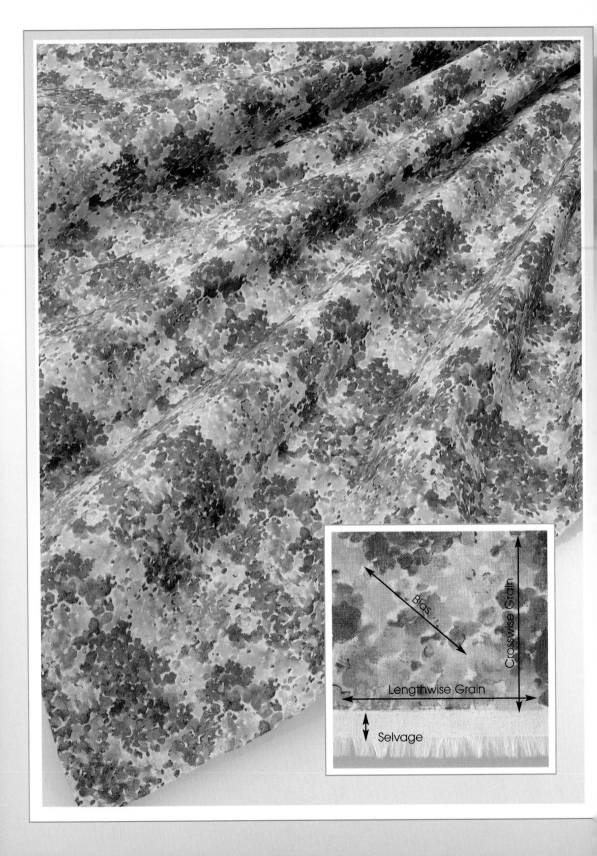

Bias

Crosswise Grain

Lengthwise Grain

Selvage

Fabric Information

After you have chosen a quilt design, it's time to select the fabric. This may seem like a difficult task at first, but consider it an adventure, and have fun. This is the time to use your vision and creativity. Just as two painters can paint the same landscape and produce very different effects, your choice of patterns, colors, and the way you combine them will give each project your unique style.

Fabrics made of 100% cotton or cotton blends can be used. Both are available in a wide variety of patterns and colors, so you'll have plenty of options to choose from. Many quilters prefer using 100% cotton fabrics because they find them easier to sew, press, mark, and hand-quilt.

If you are shopping for your fabrics in a quilt shop, they will probably be arranged according to their colors or print types, and you'll rarely find fabric that is not pure cotton. In a general fabric store, you may find a section for quilting fabrics, but there are probably other suitable fabrics located elsewhere in the store. Be sure to check the labels for fiber content and care.

The outer edges of woven fabrics are called **SELVAGES.** As a general rule, they should be trimmed away (page 31), because they are more tightly woven than the rest of the fabric, and they may shrink when laundered or pressed. **GRAINLINES** are the directions in which the fabric yarns run. Strong, stable, lengthwise yarns, running parallel to the selvages, form the **LENGTHWISE GRAIN.** The **CROSSWISE GRAIN** is perpendicular to the lengthwise grain and has a small amount of give. The diagonal direction, which has considerable stretch, is called the **BIAS.**

Prints

Printed cotton fabrics are available in a wide range of design styles and print sizes. They include batiks **(A)**, homespun plaids and florals **(B)**, tiny-grained prints that "read" as solids **(C)**, reproduction prints reminiscent of the 1930s **(D)**, and soft flannels **(E)**.

Solids

Solid-color fabrics come in a rainbow of colors, with shades and tints to suit any purpose. They include a variety of hand-dyed cottons that have a subtle sueded look. You'll often find them available in packets of graduated color values or hues. Muslin, available bleached or unbleached, is usually used for the background pieces in a design, for plain blocks, or for the quilt backing.

Backing Fabrics

The backing fabric should have the same care requirements as the fabrics in the quilt top. For smaller projects, especially when the backing is visible, back the quilt top with one of the fabrics used on the front. For wall hangings and other items where the backing is rarely seen, muslin is a good choice. If you want to accentuate the quilting stitches on the backing side, choose a solid-colored fabric. Printed fabrics tend to hide the stitches.

Preparing the Fabric

Preshrink your fabric, especially if you intend to launder the finished project. Most cotton fabrics shrink 2 to 3 percent when washed and dried, so if they're not preshrunk, the fabrics may pucker at the stitching lines and the finished size of the quilted piece may change the first time it is washed.

Launder fabrics in your washing machine on a short, warm cycle. There's no need to use detergent, but be sure to wash like colors together, in case they aren't colorfast. Check the rinse water of dark or vivid fabrics to be sure they are colorfast; if dye transfers to the water, continue rinsing the fabric until the water is clear. Machine dry the fabric until it is only slightly damp, and then press it.

Selecting Fabrics

Use contrasting colors to make the pieces of a quilt block stand out from each other. Combine warm colors (reds, yellows, or oranges) in the same quilt block with cool colors (blues, greens, or violets) to make them all seem more vivid.

Any fabric shape, whether solid-color or print, will "pop" from the quilt surface when surrounded by white or nearly white fabric.

Select a multicolor print first, perhaps for the border. Then select fabrics for the quilt block pieces, drawing colors from the print.

Interesting visual effects are achieved by using colors with graduated values (lightness or darkness). Stack all the fabrics you are considering on a table; then stand back and squint. Or view them through a special filtering tool, available at quilt shops, designed for judging **COLOR VALUES.** The filter blocks out color and reveals only the intensity of the fabric.

Combine fabrics with various print scales and styles to add visual texture to your quilt. Don't be afraid to cut up a large-scale print into smaller pieces.

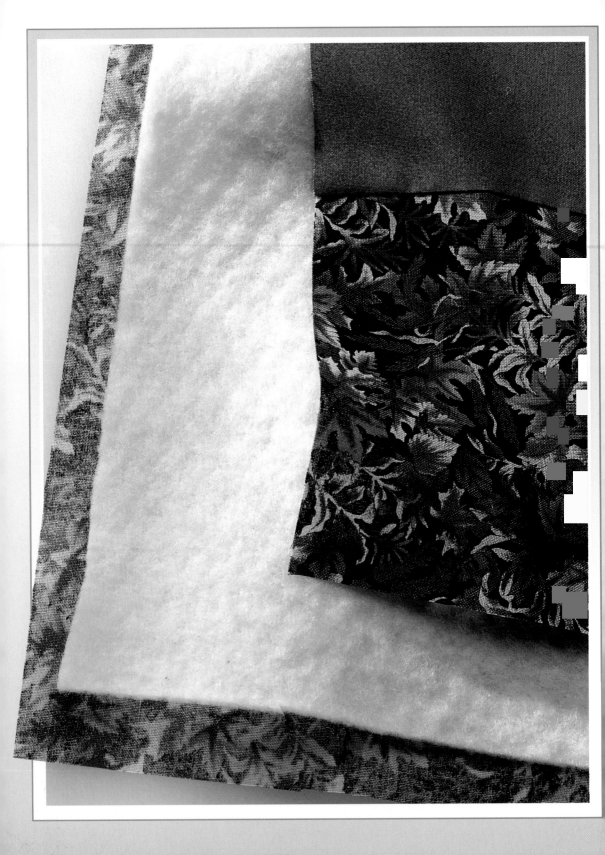

Selecting the *Batting*

Low-loft polyester batting, used in this wall hanging, is easy to machine-quilt and very durable.

The middle layer of the quilt is called the batting. When selecting batting for any project, consider the amount of **LOFT,** its drapability, and the distance required between quilting stitches to prevent the batting from bunching or pulling apart. This distance, usually ranging from 1" to 6" (2.5 to 15 cm), is printed on the package label.

Cotton, polyester, and cotton/polyester blends are the most common fibers used in batting. Cotton batting gives a flat, traditional appearance when quilted. It absorbs moisture and is cool in the summer and warm in the winter. Polyester batting is more durable, is easier to handle than cotton, and gives a slightly puffier look. It provides warmth without weight, is nonallergenic, and resists moth and mildew damage. For the traditional appearance of cotton, but the stability and ease in handling of polyester, choose a cotton/polyester blend.

Low-loft battings are recommended for machine quilting; but even low-loft battings vary in thickness. Extra-low-loft battings are often used for garments or placemats. For wall hangings or lap quilts, select a low-loft batting that is sturdy but drapable.

Batting is available in a wide range of sizes, although the selection in certain fibers and construction types may be limited. Available in quilting stores and many fabric stores, batting can be purchased by the yard and in small packages for clothing and craft projects. It is also packaged for standard-size bed quilts.

Cotton/polyester low-loft batting provides warmth, durability, and easy laundering for a cozy lap quilt.

Extra-low-loft polyester batting is a good choice for placemats or table runners, when you want a subtle quilted look for an item that may be laundered often.

Rotary Cutting

Accuracy in cutting is critical to successful quilting. A small error, multiplied by each piece, will result in blocks that don't fit together. You don't need that kind of frustration when you are learning to sew! Take the time to cut accurately, and give yourself a head start in the quilting game.

You'll find the investment in a **ROTARY CUTTER AND MAT** well worth it, once you start to use them. While indispensable for quilting, they are also perfectly suited for any other sewing project. Rotary cutting is not only a very accurate method, it also saves time. Instead of cutting each piece of the quilt individually, you can cut several identical pieces at once and have the entire project cut and ready to sew in minutes.

Straightening the Fabric

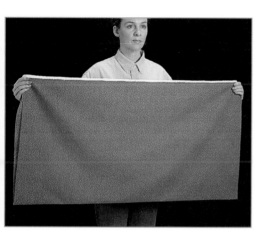

1 First, determine the **GRAINLINE.** Fold the fabric in half and hold it by the **SELVAGES.** Shift one side, if necessary, until the fabric hangs straight. The foldline is the straight **LENGTHWISE GRAIN.**

2 Lay the fabric on the cutting mat, with the fold along a grid line. Place the ruler on the fabric, close to the raw edge, at a 90° angle to the fold. Holding the ruler firmly in place with one hand, trim the excess fabric off along the edge of the ruler, using the rotary cutter. Apply steady, firm pressure to the blade. Stop when the rotary cutter gets past your hand.

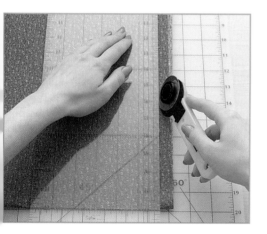

3 Leave the blade in position, and reposition your hand on the ruler ahead of the blade. Hold firmly, and continue cutting. Make sure the fabric and the ruler don't move. Shift your hand position on the ruler whenever necessary.

4 Reposition the folded fabric on the cutting mat with the straightened end on a horizontal grid line. Place the ruler over the fabric perpendicular to the cut end, with the edge just inside the selvages. Cut off the selvages, using the rotary cutter as in steps 2 and 3.

Cutting Strips

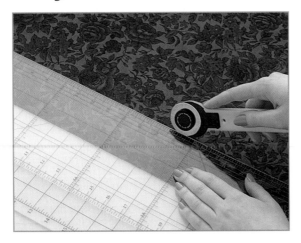

1 Position the folded fabric so that the edge you will be cutting is on the left if you are right-handed, or on the right if you are left-handed. Place the ruler on the fabric, aligning the trimmed edge with the appropriate measurement on the ruler. Holding the ruler firmly, cut as on page 31, steps 2 and 3.

2 Lift the ruler and move the cut strip so that you are able to see the cutting line. Reposition the ruler and cut the next strip.

Cutting Squares or Rectangles

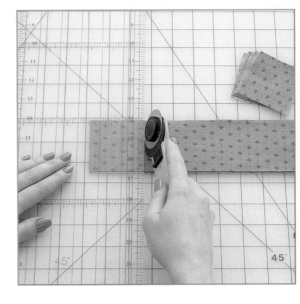
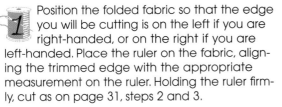

Stack three or four strips, matching the edges exactly. Place the ruler on the fabric, aligning the short edge of the fabric with the appropriate measurement on the ruler. Hold the ruler firmly in place. Cut the fabric, guiding the rotary cutter along the edge of the ruler.

TIP: These photos show you how a right-handed person would hold the ruler and rotary cutter. If you are left-handed, you would hold the tools in opposite hands and work from the opposite direction.

Cutting Triangles

Stack three or four squares, matching the edges exactly. Place the ruler over the squares diagonally, aligning it exactly to the corners of the squares. Cut through the squares, guiding the rotary cutter along the edge of the ruler. The project directions will tell you what size to cut the squares and whether to cut them diagonally once or twice.

SAFETY TIP: Because rotary cutters are extremely sharp, the manufacturers have designed ways to cover or retract the blades. <u>ALWAYS</u> use this safety feature, every time you put the tool down. An open blade falling from a table can easily slice through leather shoes. Keep your fingers out of the way when you are cutting, avoiding awkward positions where you have less control. Above all, keep the cutters in a safe place where children will not find them.

Cutting a Rectangle Wider than the Ruler

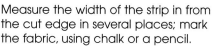

1 Measure the width of the strip in from the cut edge in several places; mark the fabric, using chalk or a pencil.

2 Align the ruler to the marks, and hold it firmly in place. Cut the fabric, guiding the rotary cutter along the edge of the ruler, over the marks.

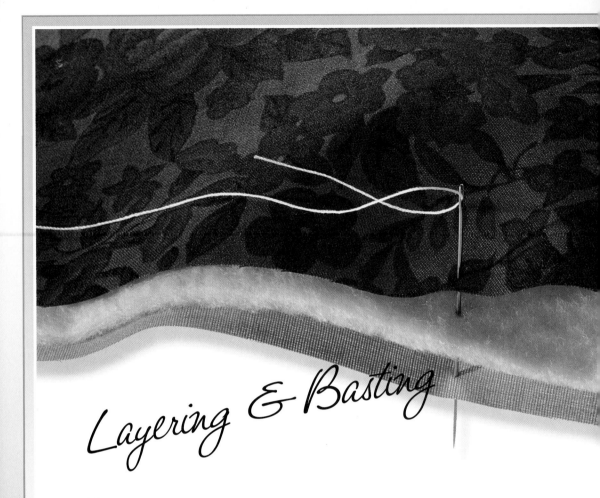

Layering & Basting

Every quilt project, from the simplest one-piece hot pad to a multi-block bed quilt, must be layered and basted before you proceed with the actual quilting stitches. Basting keeps the quilt top, batting, and backing from shifting while you are quilting. Traditionally, quilts have been basted using a hand needle and thread. While this is still a viable alternative, you may save a little time basting with safety pins. If you prefer basting with thread, use a single strand of white cotton thread and a large milliner's or darning needle. For safety-pin basting, use only rustproof pins, in either 1" or 1½" (2.5 or 3.8 cm) size. For either method, follow the same steps for layering the quilt.

Layering the Quilt

1 **PRESS** the quilt top and backing fabric flat. Mark the center of each side of the quilt top at the raw edges, using safety pins. Repeat this step for the batting and the backing. Place the backing on your work surface, wrong side up. Use masking tape to tape the backing securely to your work surface, beginning at the center of each side and working toward the corners. Keep the fabric taut but not stretched.

2 Place the batting on the backing, matching the center pins on all sides. Smooth the batting (but don't stretch it), working from the center of the quilt out to the sides.

3 Place the quilt top, right side up, over the batting, matching the pins on each side. Again, smooth the fabric without stretching it. For clarity, we are using a solid piece of fabric in place of a multicolor pieced quilt top.

Basting with Thread

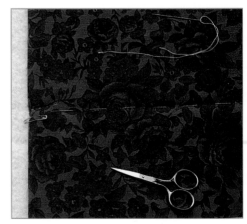

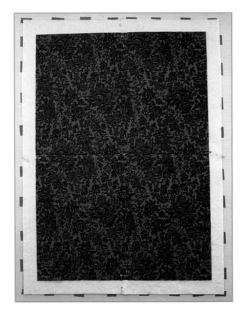

1. Thread the needle with a long strand of thread; tie a knot in the end. Begin at the center of the quilt, and stitch toward the side, taking 1" (2.5 cm) stitches through all three layers. Avoid stitching directly on seamlines or marked quilting lines. Pull the stitches snug so the layers will not shift.

2. Baste to the side of the quilt. **Backstitch** two or three stitches to secure.

3. Repeat steps 1 and 2 in each direction, so that you have divided the quilt into four quadrants with the basting stitches.

4. Baste parallel rows of stitches, no less than 6" (15 cm) apart, in one quadrant of the quilt. Work from the existing basting line toward the outer edge. Then repeat with parallel rows in the opposite direction.

TIP: As you run out of thread, back-stitch a few stitches. Then rethread the needle, knot the thread, and continue basting from where you stopped.

Backstitch. Take a few stitches in the opposite direction when you get to the end of a basting row. This will hold the basting in place but is easier to remove than a knot.

5 Repeat step 4 for each quadrant of the quilt. Remove the tape from the backing. Fold the edges of the backing over the batting and edges of the quilt top, and safety-pin them in place. This prevents the raw edges from raveling and prevents the batting from catching on the needle and feed dogs during quilting.

Basting with Safety Pins

Follow the same guidelines, first dividing the quilt into quadrants, and then working on one quadrant at a time. Insert all the pins in the same direction. Space them no more than 6" (15 cm) apart in parallel rows, vertically and horizontally. Avoid placing pins where you will be quilting.

TIP: Safety-pin basting goes more quickly if the pins are all open. In fact, they can be purchased at quilting stores already opened. Then, as you remove them from your quilt, leave them open and ready for the next project. You'll save a little wear and tear on your fingers.

Basic Quilting Techniques

Quilting holds the quilt top, batting, and backing of the quilt together. But beyond its function, quilting adds texture and interest to the quilt, enhancing its pieced design. For best effect, the quilting should reinforce or complement the piecing or appliqué design, and it should form an appealing design on the back as well as the front of the quilt.

You can quilt by hand or by machine; there are advantages to either method. Hand quilting is the traditional method, and many quilters still prefer it that way. Machine quilting, of course, takes less time and is also more durable. Whether quilting by hand or machine, your stitching should cover the surface of the quilt uniformly. This guideline is more than just an aesthetic consideration; heavily quilted areas tend to shrink more than lightly quilted ones.

WHAT YOU'LL NEED

For hand quilting:
Hand-quilting thread
Quilting needle
Thimble
Quilting frame

For machine quilting:
Walking foot
All-purpose thread or nylon
monofilament thread

Hand Quilting

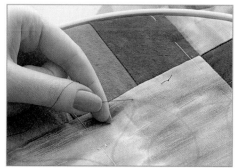

1 Center the area you will work on in your quilting frame. Thread a quilting needle with a single strand of of hand-quilting thread, about 18" (46 cm) long; tie a small knot in the end. Take one long stitch, inserting the needle from the top into the batting, about 1" (2.5 cm) from where you want to begin stitching. Don't stitch through to the backing. Bring the needle up where you will begin quilting.

2 Pull on your thread, gently "popping" the knot under the surface of the fabric. Don't pull too hard, or you'll pull the stitch out completely.

3 Take small, even stitches, up and down, through all three layers. If possible, take two to four stitches on your needle before pulling it through the quilt. Strive for quilting that looks the same on the top and the back of the quilt. The stitches should be the same length on both sides.

TIP: To avoid poking a hole in the finger that pushes the needle, you'll want to wear a thimble. Many quilters find leather thimbles more comfortable than plastic or metal.

4 To finish a row of quilting, tie a small knot close to the surface of the fabric next to your last stitch. Use your thumbnail to gently pull the fabric, again "popping" the knot under the surface of the fabric. Take a shallow stitch, and clip the thread.

TIP: While small stitches are desirable, uniformity is more important. Practice taking six stitches per inch (2.5 cm) as a beginner.

Machine Quilting

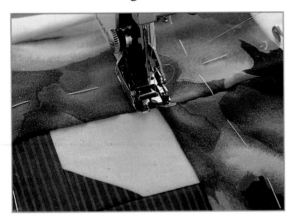

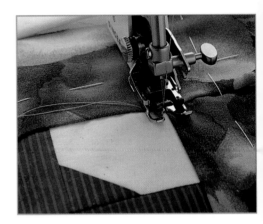

1 Attach a walking foot. Place the quilt under the foot, in the area where you will begin quilting. Lower the foot. Turn the handwheel by hand for one stitch, and stop with the needle at the highest position. Raise the foot, and pull on the needle thread to bring the bobbin thread up through the fabric.

2 Draw both threads under the walking foot to one side. Lower the walking foot, with the needle aligned to enter the fabric at the desired starting point.

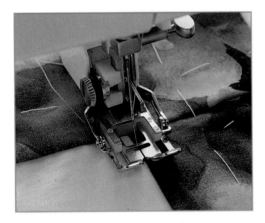

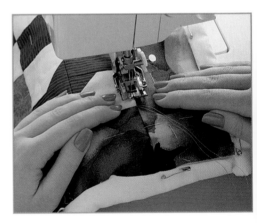

3 Stitch several very short stitches to secure the threads at the beginning of the stitching line. Gradually increase the stitch length for about 1/2" (1.3 cm), until it is the desired length; about 15 stitches per inch, which equals 2 mm.

4 Slow your stitching as you approach a stopping point. Beginning about 1/2" (1.3 cm) from the end, gradually decrease the stitch length until you are barely moving, to secure the threads.

TIP: Stitch with your hands positioned on either side of the walking foot, holding the fabric taut.

Machine-quilting Patterns

Stitch-in-the-ditch quilting emphasizes the pieced design because it is stitched following the seamlines for the blocks. Stitch so that the needle enters the well of the seam.

Channel quilting is stitched in relatively evenly spaced lines. You can mark them before you layer and baste the quilt, or for a less formal look, you can stitch them more irregularly. The quilting lines can be either diagonal, vertical, or horizontal.

Outline quilting. Stitch about 1/4″ (6 mm) away from the seamlines, guiding the edge of the walking foot along the seam.

TIP: Whenever you need to change direction, stop with the needle down in the fabric. Raise the walking foot, and **PIVOT.** Then lower the walking foot and continue stitching.

Binding

Binding is the final step for most of your quilting projects. Enclosing the edges of the quilt, the binding forms a clean, attractive finish. Binding fabrics can either match or complement the other fabrics in the quilt. Very often a quilt is bound in the same fabric as the outer border.

Binding a Quilt

1 Cut 3" (7.5 cm) binding strips from the entire crosswise width of the fabric. If the sides of your quilt are shorter than the length of the binding strips, go on to step 3. Pin two strips, right sides together, at right angles, if the sides of your quilt are longer than one binding strip. Mark a diagonal line from the corner of the upper strip to the corner of the lower strip. Stitch on the marked line.

Measure the quilt top across the middle.
After piecing and quilting a quilt top, it is likely that the top and bottom may be slightly different lengths. By making both bindings the same length as the middle of the quilt, you are able to square up the finished project.

Trim the **SEAM ALLOWANCES** to ¼" (6 mm). **PRESS** the seam open.

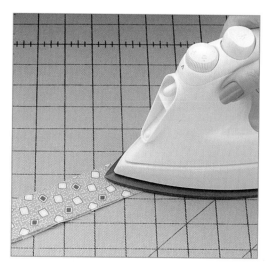

Press the binding strips in half length-wise, wrong sides together.

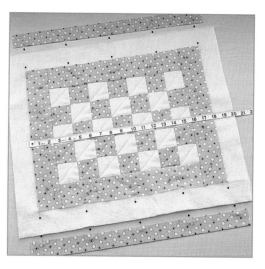

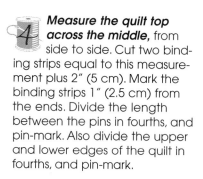

Measure the quilt top across the middle, from side to side. Cut two bind-ing strips equal to this measure-ment plus 2" (5 cm). Mark the binding strips 1" (2.5 cm) from the ends. Divide the length between the pins in fourths, and pin-mark. Also divide the upper and lower edges of the quilt in fourths, and pin-mark.

continued

Binding a Quilt *continued*

5 Pin a binding strip on the right side of the upper edge of the quilt, aligning the raw edges of the binding to the raw edge of the quilt top, and matching the pin marks. Insert the pins perpendicular to the raw edges. The binding will extend 1" (2.5 cm) beyond the quilt at each end.

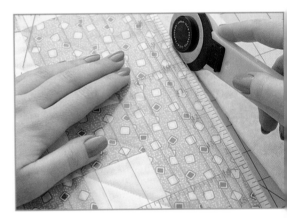

6 Stitch the binding strip to the quilt ¼" (6 mm) from the raw edges of the binding. Remove the pins as you come to them.

7 Trim off the excess batting and backing ½" (1.3 cm) from the stitching line.

8 Wrap the binding snugly around the edge of the quilt, covering the stitching line on the back of the quilt. Pin the binding in place from the right side, **inserting the pins in the well of the seam (p. 57),** parallel to the binding.

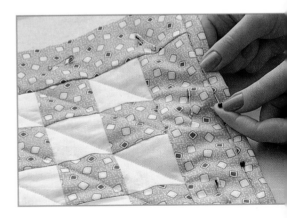

TIP: For easier removal, insert all the pins so that the heads will be toward you when you are stitching.

9 **STITCH IN THE DITCH** on the right side of the quilt, catching the binding on the back of the quilt. Remove the pins as you come to them.

10 Repeat steps 5 to 9 for the lower edge of the quilt. Trim the ends of the upper and lower binding strips even with the edges of the quilt top.

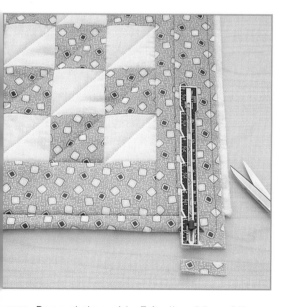

11 Repeat steps 4 to 7 for the sides of the quilt, measuring the quilt top down the middle, from top to bottom, in step 4. Trim the ends of the binding strips to extend 1/2" (1.3 cm) beyond the finished edges of the quilt.

12 Wrap and pin the binding around the edge, as in step 8. At each end, fold in the raw edges of the binding. Then fold under the 1/2" (1.3 cm) end; press. Finish wrapping and pinning the binding. Stitch the binding as in step 9.

Raw-edge Appliqué
Hot Pad

Raw-edge **APPLIQUÉS** add dimension and interest to a quilted project. Practice the technique by creating this maple leaf hot pad. Because the batting is quite thin, these hot pads are more decorative than useful. The edges of the leaf can be frayed with a stiff brush. For minimal fraying, use a tightly woven fabric for the appliqué. If you would like a more natural frayed look, machine wash and tumble dry the hot pad. The finished hot pad is about 9" (23 cm) square.

WHAT YOU'LL LEARN

How to sew a raw-edge appliqué

How to channel-quilt

WHAT YOU'LL NEED

3/8 yd. (0.35 m) background fabric, for the hot pad

1/4 yd. (0.25 m) contrasting fabric, for the appliqué and binding

Low-loft batting, about 13" (33 cm) square

ROTARY CUTTER AND MAT

Quilting ruler

Thread to match or blend with the fabrics

Glue stick

Decorative ring

Let's Begin

1 Straighten the cut ends of the fabric, and trim off the **SELVAGES** (page 31). Cut a 9" (23 cm) square of background fabric for the hot pad front. Cut a 13" (33 cm) square of background fabric for the back. Cut a 13" (33 cm) square of batting. Cut four 3" x 11" (7.5 x 28 cm) strips of contrasting fabric for the binding. **Cut a leaf appliqué** from the contrasting fabric, about 6" (15 cm) wide.

2 *Glue-baste* the leaf appliqué, right side up, to the right side of the hot pad front. Position the leaf as desired in the center of the square.

Quick Reference

Cut a leaf appliqué. Draw a pattern freehand, or trace around a real leaf. Because the edges will not be finished in any way, avoid any long narrow extensions or small details that could ravel away entirely.

Glue-baste. Using a glue stick, apply dots of glue to the wrong side of the appliqué. This will hold it temporarily in place until you catch it permanently to the hot pad with quilting stitches.

Stopping with the needle down in the fabric. Stop running the machine with the foot pedal. Turn the handwheel on your machine manually until the needle is all the way down into the fabric.

3 Layer and baste the hot pad (page 34). Remove the layers from the work surface. Attach a walking foot (page 9), if you have one. Set your stitch length at 12 stitches per inch, which equals 2.5 mm. Begin stitching in the upper right corner of the pad, about 1" (2.5 cm) from the cut edge of the top layer.

4 Stitch from top to bottom, *stopping with the needle down in the fabric.* Lift the presser foot, **PIVOT** the hot pad 90°, and lower the presser foot. Stitch about 1" (2.5 cm). Stopping with the needle down, lift the presser foot, and pivot the hot pad another 90°, to begin a new row of stitching.

continued

continued

5 Repeat this process until the entire hot pad is channel-quilted, catching the leaf appliqué in the stitching. If you basted the hot pad with safety pins, remove them as you come to them.

TIP: Relax! The rows of channel quilting don't need to be perfectly parallel. In fact, some variation is desirable to give it handmade charm.

6 Bind the edges of the hot pad, following the directions on page 42. Hand-stitch a small decorative ring to one corner, for hanging, if desired.

Variations
ON THE THEME

Make hot pads for all seasons. Stitch a fir tree appliqué over a snowy print fabric for a winter hot pad. Get in the Halloween spirit with fall colors and a pumpkin appliqué. Or how about a spring fever hot pad?

Nine-patch Pillow

This charming pillow for your bedroom or living room is made by stitching nine squares of fabric together in a checkerboard pattern. You'll need to select two coordinating prints, a coordinating print and solid, or two contrasting solids. The checkerboard pattern is repeated on the back side of the pillow, with the squares arranged in the reverse order.

WHAT YOU'LL LEARN

The importance
of accuracy
in both cutting
and stitching

Tricks for perfectly
matched seams

How to
STITCH IN THE DITCH

WHAT YOU'LL NEED

½ yd. (0.5 m)
each of two
coordinating fabrics

⅝ yd. (0.6 m) muslin, for
the pillow backing

⅝ yd. (0.6 m) batting

**ROTARY CUTTER
AND MAT**

Quilting ruler

Thread to match or
blend with the fabrics

18" (46 cm)
square pillow form

Let's Begin

1 Straighten the cut ends of the fabrics, and trim off the **SELVAGES** (page 31). With the fabric still folded in half, cut two 6½" (16.3 cm) strips of fabric across the entire width, from the cut edges to the fold.

2 Cut nine 6½" (16.3 cm) squares from these strips.

3 Repeat steps 1 and 2 for fabric B. Arrange the squares in two nine-patch blocks, as shown.

1/4" (6 mm) seam allowance guide.
For many machines, this means guiding the fabric along the edge of the presser foot. With your machine set for straight stitching, measure 1/4" (6 mm) from the tip of the needle to the right. Mark a guideline with narrow tape on the throat plate.

4 Pin one A square to one B square along one side, with right sides together. Align the cut ends and edges. Place the fabric under the presser foot, aligning the upper edges to the needle hole in the throat plate. Align the cut edges of the fabric to the **1/4" (6 mm) seam allowance guide** on your machine. Stitch a 1/4" (6 mm) **SEAM**, removing pins as you come to them.

TIP: As tempting as it may be, don't sew over pins! You may be lucky and save a few seconds, but sooner or later your needle will break, costing you much more time in the long run.

5 Pin another A square to the opposite side of the B square. Stitch a 1/4" (6 mm) seam, forming a three-square strip.

continued

continued

6 Repeat steps 4 and 5 to make two more identical three-square strips. Then sew the remaining strips together, with an A square in the center of each. *Press* the **SEAM ALLOWANCES** toward the darker squares. The strips should now measure 6½" x 18½" (16.3 x 47.3 cm).

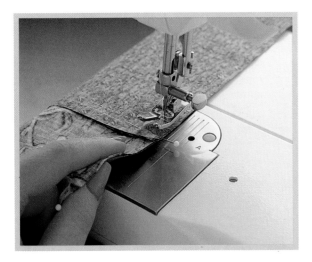

7 Beginning with the pillow front, pin the top strip to the center strip, with right sides together and raw edges even. Align the seams, *inserting pins in the wells of the seams.* You will notice that the matching seam allowances turn in opposite directions. Stitch a ¼" (6 mm) seam, removing pins as you come to them.

TIP: To ensure smooth seams and perfect inter-sections, slow down as you approach each one. Stop with the needle down in the fabric, raise the presser foot, and lift the strips slightly from the machine bed. Make sure the seam allowances on the underside are still turned in the direction they were pressed. Then lower the presser foot and continue sewing.

8 Pin the remaining strip to the opposite side of the center strip, pinning as in step 7; stitch the seam. You have just completed a nine-patch block. Press both seam allowances away from the center.

Press. Remember that "press" means to lift the iron to move it to a new position. Avoid sliding the iron, which can stretch fabric out of shape.

Insert pins in the wells of the seams. By pinning in this manner, you are making sure that the stitched seams will line up perfectly on the right side of the pillow. Stitch up to these pins as close as you can before removing them.

9 Repeat steps 7 and 8 for the pillow back. Cut two squares of muslin and two squares of batting, each 4" (10 cm) larger than the pillow front and back. Layer and baste the front and back (page 34).

10 Remove the layers from the work surface. Set your stitch length at 10 to 12 stitches per inch, which equals 2.5 mm. Attach a walking foot (page 9), if you have one, or use an all-purpose presser foot. Quilt each block, using the stitch-in-the-ditch method (page 41) along all the seams.

11 Set your stitch length to long, and machine-baste around the pillow top a scant 1/4" (6 mm) from the edge of the top fabric. Trim the batting and muslin even with the edges of the top fabric, using a rotary cutter and mat. Repeat for the pillow back.

continued

continued

12 Place the pillow back over the pillow front, with right sides together, matching the raw edges. Align the seams of the front block to the corresponding seams of the back block. Insert pins in the wells of the seams.

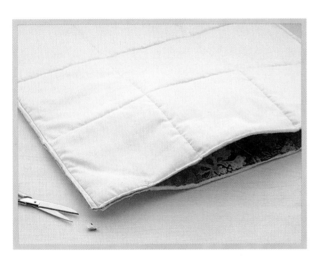

13 Stitch around the pillow cover, 1/4" (6 mm) from the raw edges, leaving a 10" (25.5 cm) opening along one side. Trim the corners diagonally, to remove excess bulk.

14 Turn the pillow cover right side out through the opening. Use a point turner or similar tool to carefully push the corners out, if necessary. Insert the pillow form into the pillow cover. Pin the opening closed. Slipstitch the opening closed, alternating small stitches from one side of the opening to the other as shown.

Variations
ON THE THEME

Tie the pillow cover instead of stitch-in-the-ditch quilting. Thread a tapestry needle with a 1/16" (1.5 mm) ribbon. Take a 1/4" (6 mm) stitch diagonally across one of the four center seam intersections of the pillow cover. Tie the ribbon ends on the right side, and trim the ribbon ends to the desired length. Repeat this in the other three center seam intersections, and for those on the pillow back.

Use different solids of the same color for a more subtle look. Add interest and texture with diagonal rows of quilting stitches through the squares. Mark the diagonal lines before layering and basting the pillow pieces.

Checkerboard Placemats

Add homespun charm to your dining table with this set of four checkerboard placemats. Select two coordinating print fabrics, a print and a solid, or two solids, preferably with a high contrast between them. Then make quick-and-easy napkins to match.

The directions are for four placemats. You will find that this **STRIP-PIECING** method of construction saves time in sewing and cuts down on the number of trips back and forth to the ironing board. Set your machine for a straight stitch of 10 to 12 stitches per inch, which equals 2.5 mm, and sew ¼" (6 mm) **SEAM ALLOWANCES** throughout the entire project. Each finished placemat measures about 14" x 18" (35.5 x 46 cm).

WHAT YOU'LL LEARN

Strip piecing saves time

How to add a border to your quilt project

How to sew **DOUBLE-FOLD HEMS** on napkins

WHAT YOU'LL NEED

½ yd. (0.5 m) light-colored print or solid fabric, we'll call "A"

2 yd. (1.85 m) darker-colored print or solid fabric, we'll call "B"

Additional fabric, for napkins (A or B)

Low-loft polyester or poly/cotton blend batting

ROTARY CUTTER AND MAT

Quilting ruler

Thread to match fabric A

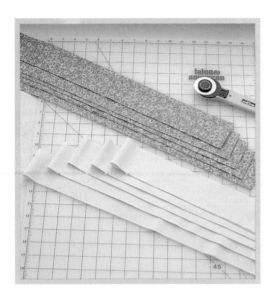

Let's Begin

1 Straighten the cut ends of the fabrics, and trim off the **SELVAGES** (page 31). Cut five 2¹/2" (6.5 cm) strips from the entire crosswise width of fabric A. Cut five 2¹/2" (6.5 cm) strips from the entire crosswise width of fabric B.

2 Cut seven 2¹/2" (6.5 cm) strips from the entire crosswise width of fabric B, for the border. Cut seven 3" (7.5 cm) strips from the entire crosswise width of fabric B, for the binding.

3 Pin an A strip and a B strip right sides together, aligning the long edges; insert the pins perpendicular to the long edge. Stitch the strips together, removing the pins as you come to them. Then stitch another A strip to the other side of the B strip, in the same manner. Continue adding strips, alternating fabrics, until you have three A strips and two B strips. **PRESS** the seam allowances toward the darker fabric (B).

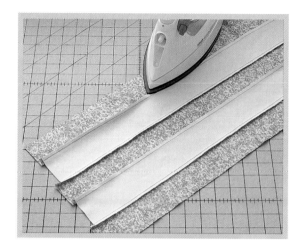

 Stitch three B strips and two A strips together, as in step 3, with fabrics alternating in the opposite sequence. Press the seam allowances toward the darker fabric (B).

Cut the pieced strip sets, perpendicular to the seams, into 2½" (6.5 cm) strips.

TIP: If your fabric is 45" (115 cm) wide, you should be able to cut at least seventeen small strips from each set. You will need sixteen of one set and twelve of the other to complete four placemats.

Align the raw edges of two different strips, right sides together, matching the seams. The seam allowances will be pressed in opposite directions. **Insert a pin in the well of the seams (p. 57),** to make sure they line up exactly. Stitch the strips together, removing the pins as you come to them and keeping the seam allowances turned in opposite directions.

continued

continued

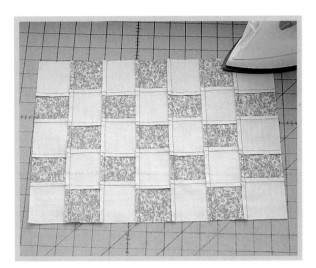

7 Add five more strips as in step 6, alternating patterns, for a total of seven strips. Press all the new seam allowances in the same direction.

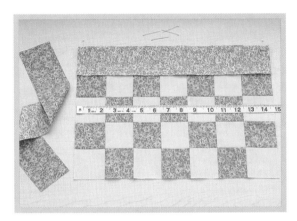

8 Measure the placemat lengthwise across the center. Cut two border strips equal to this measurement. Pin one strip to the top of the placemat; pin the other strip to the bottom. Align the ends of the strips to the sides of the placemat. Stretch the strips or the placemat slightly, if necessary, to make them fit. Stitch 1/4" (6 mm) seams; press the seam allowances toward the borders.

9 Measure the placemat widthwise across the center, including the new borders. Cut two border strips equal to this measurement. Pin a strip to each side of the placemat, aligning the ends of the strips to the top and bottom edges of the placemat. Stretch the strips or the placemat slightly, if necessary, to make them fit. Stitch 1/4" (6 mm) seams; press the seam allowances toward the borders.

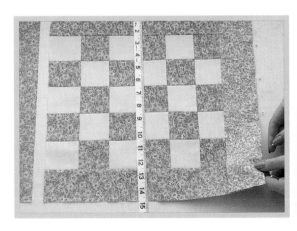

Quick Reference

Following this sequence. By quilting in this sequence, you first anchor the quilt vertically and horizontally, preventing the layers from shifting.

10 Repeat steps 6 to 9 for the three other placemats. Cut the backing fabric and batting 4" (10 cm) longer and wider than the placemat. Layer and baste the placemats (page 34).

11 Attach a walking foot (page 9). Quilt by **STITCHING IN THE DITCH** (page 41), *following this sequence.* Begin with a vertical seam near the center, then a horizontal seam near the center. Then stitch in the ditch of the seam between the border and pieced section. Finish by stitching the remaining vertical seams between rows and the remaining horizontal seams between rows. Bind each placemat, following the directions on page 42.

Let's Begin

1 Cut squares for the napkins 1" (2.5 cm) larger than the desired finished size. Press under ½" (1.3 cm) on each side of the napkin. Unfold the corner, and refold it diagonally so that the pressed folds match. Press the diagonal fold, and trim the corner as shown. Repeat for each corner.

TIP: For the most efficient use of your fabric, cut three 15" (38 cm) squares from 45" (115 cm) fabric or 18" (46 cm) squares from 54" (137 cm) fabric.

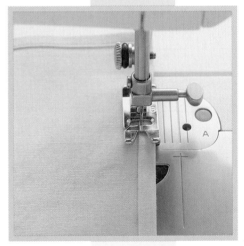

2 Fold the raw edges under to meet the pressed fold, forming a double-fold hem. The corners will form neat diagonal folds. Press the folds; pin only if necessary.

3 Stitch the hem close to the inner fold, using a short straight stitch and beginning along one side. At the corners, stop with the needle down in the fabric, between the diagonal folds, and **PIVOT.** Overlap the stitches about ½" (1.3 cm) where they meet.

More Placemat Ideas

Quilt the checkerboard pattern in diagonal rows. Simply follow a path from corner to corner. Try to

stitch continually from edge to edge as long as possible without stopping and cutting the thread.

Paint a design in the corner of each napkin, taking inspiration from the printed fabric used in the placemat. Use fabric paints; follow the manufacturer's directions for setting the paint.

Double Nine-patch
Table Topper

The double nine-patch block is a popular variation of the nine-patch block, found on page 53. This pattern alternates one-piece squares and checkerboard squares. Each of the checkerboard squares is made from nine smaller squares. The blocks are set off by **SASHING,** another popular quilting technique.

This table topper can be made in any color scheme for holiday or every-day use. Choose a low-loft batting so the finished piece lies relatively flat on your table. All **SEAM ALLOWANCES** throughout the project are 1/4" (6 mm). The finished size is about 40" (102 cm) square.

WHAT YOU'LL LEARN

How to add sashing
to the design
of your quilt top

How to quilt diagonally

The importance of
accuracy in both
cutting and stitching

WHAT YOU'LL NEED

5/8 yd. (0.6 m) fabric A, for small squares in the double nine-patch blocks and for the sashing squares (red)

2 2/3 yd. (2.48 m) fabric B, for other small squares in double nine-patch blocks, for larger squares in double nine-patch, and for backing (white)

7/8 yd. (0.8 m) fabric C, for sashing strips and binding (blue)

Low-loft batting, about 44" (112 cm) square

ROTARY CUTTER AND MAT

Quilting ruler

Thread

Let's Begin

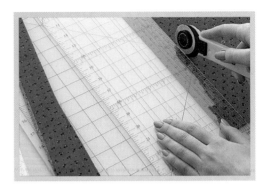

1 Straighten the cut ends of the fabrics, and trim off the **SELVAGES** (page 31). Cut ten 1¹/2" (3.8 cm) strips from the entire crosswise width of fabric A. Cut eight 1¹/2" (3.8 cm) strips from the entire crosswise width of fabric B.

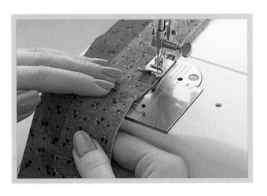

2 Pin an A strip and a B strip right sides together, aligning the long edges; insert the pins perpendicular to the long edge. Stitch the strips together, removing the pins as you come to them. Then stitch another A strip to the other side of the B strip, in the same manner.

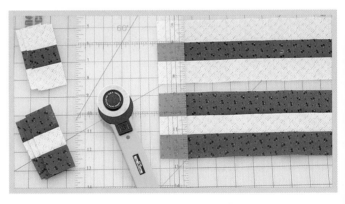

3 Repeat step 2 until you have four sets of A-B-A strips. Then make two sets of B-A-B strips, in the same manner. **PRESS** all the seam allowances toward the darker fabric (A).

4 Cut the pieced strip sets perpendicular to the seams, into 1¹/2" (3.8 cm) strips.

TIP: If your fabric is 45" (115 cm) wide, you should be able to cut at least 28 small strips from each set. You will need 90 of one set and 45 of the other to complete the table topper.

5 Align the long edge of an A-B-A strip to the long edge of a B-A-B strip, right sides together, matching the seams. The seam allowances will be pressed in opposite directions. ***Insert a pin in the well of the seams (p. 57),*** to make sure they line up exactly. Stitch the strips together, removing the pins as you come to them and keeping the seam allowances turned in the opposite directions. Stitch another A-B-A strip to the opposite side of the B-A-B strip in the same manner.

6 Repeat step 5 until you have made 45 pieced squares. Press the seams on each square toward the outside edges.

7 Cut three 3½" (9 cm) strips from the entire crosswise width of fabric B. Then cut these strips into 3½" (9 cm) squares. You will need 36 squares in all.

continued

continued

8 Stitch the pieced squares and the whole squares together in three-square strips. You'll need 18 strips that have pieced squares at the ends and nine strips that have whole squares at the ends. Press all the seam allowances toward the whole squares.

9 Stitch the strips for a double nine-patch block together, arranging them as shown. Take the time to insert a pin in the well of the seams, to ensure perfect seam intersections. Repeat this step until you have made nine double nine-patch blocks. Press the new seam allowances away from the center.

10 Cut six 3½" (9 cm) strips from the entire crosswise width of fabric C, for the sashing. *Measure the sides of several blocks to determine the shortest measurement.* Then cut the sashing into 24 strips with this length.

11 Cut two 3½" (9 cm) strips from the entire crosswise width of fabric A. Then cut the A strips into 3½" (9 cm) **connecting squares;** you'll need 16. Arrange the blocks, sashing strips, and connecting squares on a flat surface, as shown.

Quick Reference

Measure the sides of several blocks to determine the shortest measurement. Ideally, the blocks should measure 9½" (24.3 cm), but there are likely to be slight variances in seam allowance depths as you piece the blocks together. By cutting all the sashing strips to the same measurement, however, you will be able to "correct" the variances and square up the table topper.

Connecting squares. Sometimes sashing strips travel uninterrupted from one side of the quilt to the other. However, in this project, the sashing is made up of short pieces, alternating with contrasting squares. These squares "connect" pieces of the sashing in both directions, while adding an interesting design element to the overall pieced pattern of the table topper.

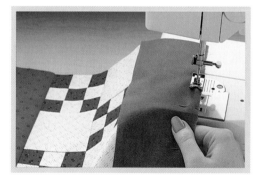

12 Stitch the first horizontal row of sashing strips and blocks together, taking the pieces in order from the surface. Align the ends of the strips to the upper and lower edges of the blocks, easing the blocks to fit as necessary. It is easiest to stitch with the sashing strip up, keeping the seam allowances of the pieced block turned in the direction they were pressed.

TIP: Use pins if you feel it would give you more control.

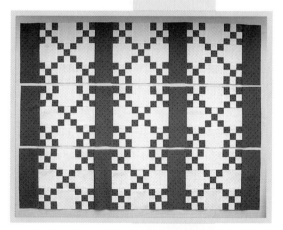

13 Repeat step 12 until you have pieced all three rows. Press all the seam allowances toward the sashing strips. Return the sashed block rows to the surface.

continued

continued

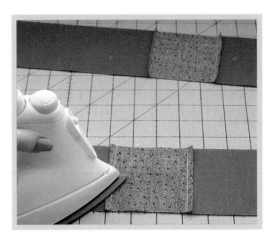

14 Stitch the horizontal rows of sashing strips and connecting squares together, taking the pieces in order from the surface. Press all the seam allowances toward the sashing strips. Return the sashing units to the surface between the sashed block rows.

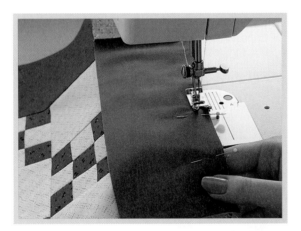

15 Place the bottom sashing unit along the lower edge of the bottom sashed block row, with right sides together, matching the seams. Insert pins in the wells of the seams, easing in any fullness. Stitch the rows together, stitching with the sashing unit facing up and removing the pins as you come to them. Take care to keep all the seam allowances turned in the direction they were pressed.

16 Continue joining the sashing units and sashed block rows, as in step 15, taking the pieces in order from the surface, until you have completed the entire table topper. Press all the seams toward the sashing units.

17 Place the table topper on a flat surface. With a quilting ruler and fabric marker, lightly mark diagonal quilting lines, bisecting the center of each double nine-patch block and running off the edge. Cut the backing fabric and batting 4" (10 cm) longer and wider than the table topper. Layer and baste the table topper as on page 34.

Quick Reference

Stitching diagonally means you are stitching on the **BIAS** and the fabric has much more give. A walking foot (page 9) is important here, in order to avoid puckers. Spacing your basting stitches or safety pins closer together will help, too.

TIP: This marking step is much easier (and more accurate) to do now, before layering and basting, because the fabric is relatively flat and smooth. If you think you can "eyeball" the quilting lines that cut diagonally through the squares, simply mark the lines where they cross the connecting squares.

18 Attach a walking foot (page 9). Machine-quilt, following the marked lines. Begin by **stitching diagonally** through the center, first in one direction and then in the other. Finish by stitching the remaining diagonal rows. Cut four 3" (7.5 cm) strips from the entire crosswise width of fabric C, for the binding. Bind the topper, following the directions on page 42.

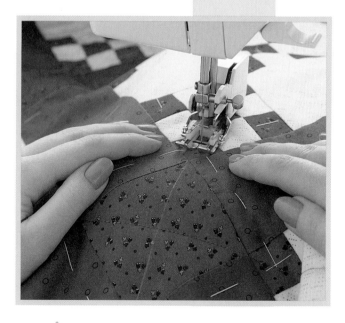

Pieced Sashing
Table Runner

This table runner, with pieced **SASHING** and quilted motifs, will add a personal decorating touch to your dining room table. The motifs in the center of each square offer an opportunity to practice quilting by hand (page 39). The sashing is made of four hand-dyed fabrics with graduated **COLOR VALUES** from light to dark. These are often sold in quilt shops, already cut into 18" (46 cm) squares called **FAT QUARTERS.** Select a print fabric for the large center squares and the ***connecting squares (p. 73)*** of the sashing. Then select four graduating colors that accent the print.

The finished size is approximately 52" x 16" (132 x 40.5 cm). All **SEAM ALLOWANCES** for this project are ¼" (6 mm). Select machine-quilting thread in a color to match or blend with the fabrics; select hand-quilting thread (page 20) in a contrasting color.

WHAT YOU'LL LEARN

How to select and use fabrics in graduated color values

How to make pieced sashing

How to make your own quilting template

Hand-quilting techniques

WHAT YOU'LL NEED

2 yd. (1.85 m) printed fabric A for large blocks, connecting squares in sashing, backing, and binding

Four hand-dyed fabrics in fat quarters, or ¼ yd. (0.25 m) each of four full-width fabrics in graduated color values, for the sashing

Low-loft batting, about 56" x 20" (142 x 51 cm)

ROTARY CUTTER AND MAT

Quilting ruler

Thread for machine quilting; thread for hand quilting

Let's Begin

1 Straighten the cut edges of your fabrics, and trim off the **SELVAGES** (page 31). Cut four 8½" (21.8 cm) squares from fabric A; also cut ten 4½" (11.5 cm) squares from fabric A. Cut 2½" (6.5 cm) strips from the entire crosswise width of each of the remaining fabrics; you'll need four strips of each if they are fat quarters or two strips of each if they are 45" (115 cm) wide.

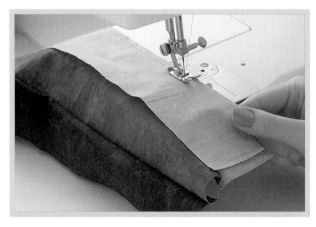

2 Arrange the strips of graduated colors in order from darkest to lightest. Place one strip from the first stack, right sides together, over a strip from the second stack, aligning the long edges. Stitch the strips together. Continue adding strips in graduated sequence from darkest to lightest.

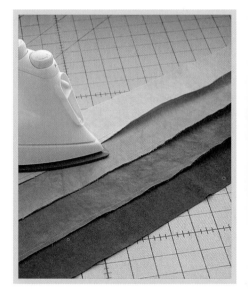

TIP: You can sew these strips together without pinning first, if you take your time. Keep the edges aligned and hold both strips with even tension. The strips may not be exactly the same length. Start with the ends evenly aligned and begin stitching from that same end with each additional strip.

3 Sew the remaining strips into sets like the first one. **PRESS** all the seam allowances toward the darker fabric.

4 Cut the pieced fabric crosswise into 4½" (11.5 cm) strips. You will need a total of 13 pieced sashing strips.

5 Arrange all of the pieces on a flat surface, and step back for a long look. There are many ways you might turn the sashing strips, causing the gradation of color to change direction. You may prefer an arrangement different from the one we have selected.

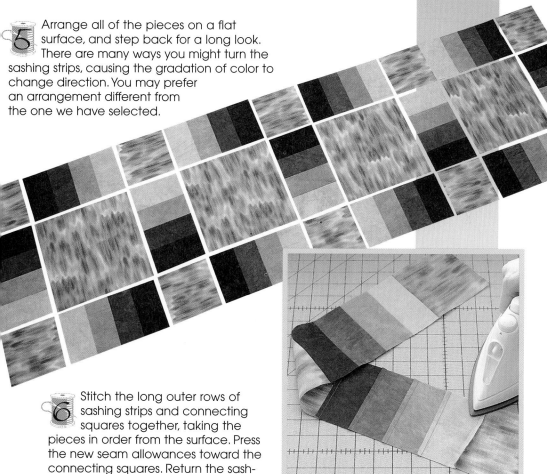

6 Stitch the long outer rows of sashing strips and connecting squares together, taking the pieces in order from the surface. Press the new seam allowances toward the connecting squares. Return the sashing units to the surface.

continued

continued

7 Stitch the center row of sashing strips and large squares together, taking the pieces in order from the surface. Press the new seam allowances toward the squares.

TIP: Pin these pieces together first, one seam at a time, if you prefer. Stitch with the square on top, taking care to keep the seam allowances of the pieced strip turned in the direction they were pressed.

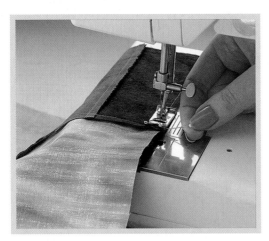

8 Place the bottom sashing row along the lower edge of the center row, with right sides together, matching the seams. The seam allowances will be pressed in opposite directions at the seam intersections. **Insert a pin in the well of the seams (p. 57),** to make sure they line up exactly. Stitch the rows together, removing the pins as you come to them and keeping the seam allowances turned in the proper directions.

9 Stitch the remaining sashing row to the other side of the center row, as in step 8. Press these long seam allowances toward the center row.

Fabric marker. Use air-erasable marker if you are able to complete the hand quilting within the next day, before the marks disappear. Otherwise use a quilting pencil or water-erasable marker.

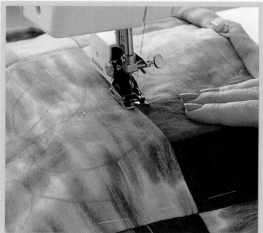

10 Cut a quilting template of the desired shape from heavy paper, approximately 2½" (6.5 cm) tall and wide. Center the template in a connecting square. Trace lightly around the pattern, using a **fabric marker**. Repeat for each of the connecting squares. Trace four intertwined motifs in each large square.

11 Cut the backing and batting 4" (10 cm) longer and wider than the table runner. Layer and baste the table runner (page 34). Quilt by machine, **STITCHING IN THE DITCH** (page 41) of the lengthwise sashing seams and all the crosswise seams that run edge to edge. Use a walking foot.

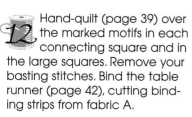

12 Hand-quilt (page 39) over the marked motifs in each connecting square and in the large squares. Remove your basting stitches. Bind the table runner (page 42), cutting binding strips from fabric A.

MORE
Table Runner
IDEAS

You can create a table runner for any special occasion. Experiment and develop your own quilting templates, or select from a wide range of templates available at quilting shops.

Select four sashing colors drawn from the multicolored print used in the large and small squares.

Try your hand at selecting small print fabrics in graduated color values for the sashing. Use a value tester (page 26), available at quilt shops, to help you choose.

Hand-quilt the entire table runner, if you prefer. Instead of machine stitching in the ditch, quilt by hand ¼" (6 mm) inside the seam around each large square.

Log Cabin Sewing Machine Cover

Designed to fit most standard sewing machines, this cover features the ever-popular Log Cabin quilt block pattern. Eight Log Cabin blocks form the front, top, and back of the cover.

To create an interesting visual effect in the Log Cabin pattern, select two sets of contrasting colors, three of one and four of the other, in **COLOR VALUES** that progress from dark to light. They can be small prints, solids, or a mixture of both. In the diagram at left, note how the color values, moving from the outer rectangles inward, progress from dark to light. The lightest fabric in the center square is also used for the side borders, ends, and binding of the sewing machine cover.

CHAINSTITCHING methods are used for quick and easy piecing of the eight blocks. All of the **SEAM ALLOWANCES** for the project are 1/4" (6 mm).

WHAT YOU'LL LEARN

How to make color values work for visual effect in a quilt pattern

Chainstitching methods for quick and easy piecing of several identical blocks

The importance of accuracy in cutting and piecing

WHAT YOU'LL NEED

1 1/4 yd. (1.15 m) fabric A for borders, backing, binding, and center squares

1/8 yd. (0.15 m) fabrics B, C, and D; 1/4 yd. (0.25 m) fabrics E, F, and G, as described above

Low-loft batting, about 20" x 32" (51 x 81.5 cm)

ROTARY CUTTER AND MAT

Quilting ruler

Thread to blend with the fabrics

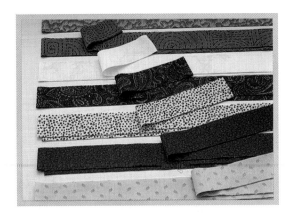

Let's Begin

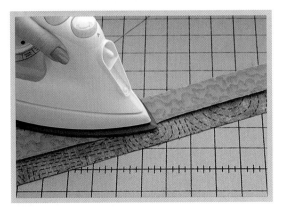

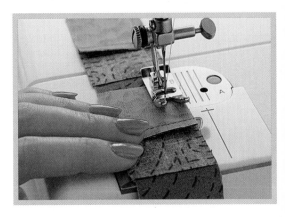

1 Straighten the cut ends of the fabrics, and trim away the **SELVAGES** (page 31). Cut 1½" (3.8 cm) strips from the entire crosswise width of each fabric; you will need one strip of A, two strips of B, C, and D, three strips of E, F, and G. Arrange the strips in the order they will be used, from A to G, as in the diagram (page 84).

2 Place strip A over strip B, right sides together, aligning the long edges. Stitch the strips together, keeping the edges aligned and holding both strips with even tension; they may not be exactly the same length. **PRESS** the seam allowances toward strip B.

3 Cut across the pieced strip at 1½" (3.8 cm) intervals, cutting eight sets. The lighter square of each of these sets will become the center of each Log Cabin block.

4 Place one set over a B strip, right sides together, aligning the ends and long edges. Position the set so that the A square is at the top; the seam allowance is turned down. Stitch them together. Without removing the fabric from the machine, place another set over the strip, aligning the edges and leaving a small space between sets. Stitch the second set in place.

5 Continue adding sets, leaving small spaces between them, until you have sewn all eight sets to the B strip. Place the pieced strip on the cutting mat, with the B strip on the bottom. Cut the sets apart, cutting the B strip even with the cut edges of the sets.

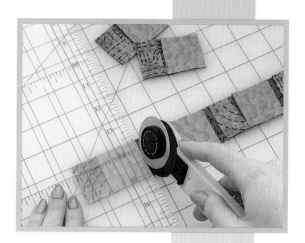

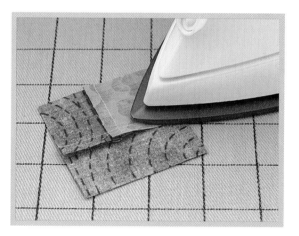

6 Press the seam allowances away from the center (A) squares.

7 Stitch a three-piece set to a C strip in the same manner. Position the set so that the most recently added rectangle is on the bottom; you will be crossing the most recently stitched seam, keeping those seam allowances turned away from the center square. Continue adding sets, leaving small spaces between them, until you have sewn all eight sets to the C strip.

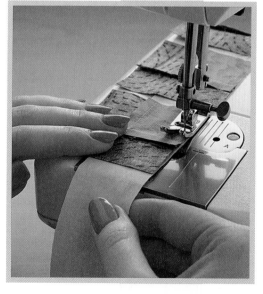

continued

continued

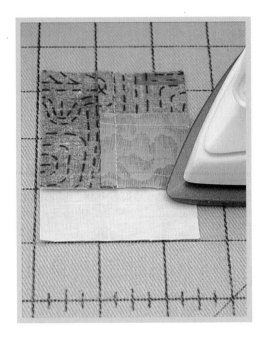

8 Place the pieced strip on the cutting mat, with the C strip on the bottom. Cut the sets apart, cutting the C strip even with the edges of the three-piece sets. Press the seam allowances away from the center (A) squares.

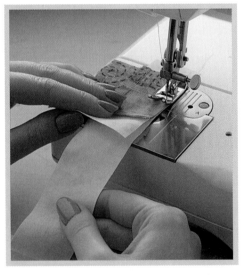

9 Stitch a four-piece set to a C strip in the same manner. Position the set so that the most recently added rectangle is on the bottom; you will be crossing the most recently stitched seam, keeping those seam allowances turned away from the center square.

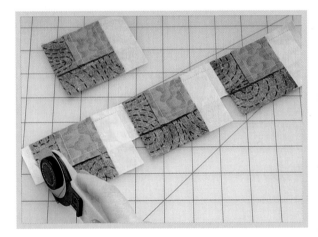

10 Continue adding sets, leaving small spaces between them, until you have sewn all eight sets to the C strip. Place the pieced strip on the cutting mat, with the C strip on the bottom. Cut the sets apart, cutting the C strip even with the edges of the four-piece sets. Press the seam allowances away from the center.

11 Have you got the idea? Continue building the blocks with this chainstitching method, adding two rectangles of each fabric in turn. Refer to the diagram on page 84 if you get confused. Sew accurate 1/4" (6 mm) seams. Your squares should measure 7 1/2" (19.3 cm).

TIP: At any point, if you run out of strip length, take another strip of the same fabric and continue piecing.

12 Arrange all of the pieces on a flat surface, and step back for a long look. There are a few different ways you might turn the blocks to get the visual effect you want. Follow our example, or create a new pattern of your own.

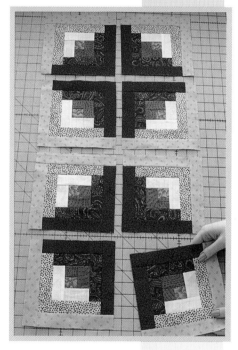

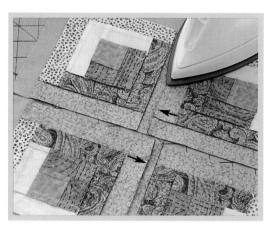

13 Stitch each two-block row together. You may find it helpful to pin first, before stitching. Press the seam allowances in alternating directions from row to row.

continued

continued

14 Place the bottom two rows right sides together, matching the center seams. ***Insert pins in the wells of the seams (p. 57).*** Stitch the rows together, easing in any fullness; remove the pins as you come to them. Take care to keep all the seam allowances turned in the direction they were pressed. Add the remaining rows, one at a time. Your pieced section should measure 28½" x 14½" (72.3 x 36.8 cm).

15 Cut two 5½" (14 cm) strips from the entire crosswise width of fabric A. Cut the strips into two 28½" (72.3 cm) lengths for the side borders. Pin one strip to each side of the pieced section. Align the ends of the strips to the ends of the section, easing them to fit. Stitch ¼" (6 mm) seams; press the seam allowances toward the borders. Mark lines for channel quilting (page 41) 1" (2.5 cm) apart on the borders, beginning 1" (2.5 cm) from the seam. The last lines will be ¼" (6 mm) from the edge.

16 Cut the backing fabric and the batting 4" (10 cm) longer and wider than the pieced fabric. Layer and baste the pieced fabric, as on page 34. Quilt by machine, **STITCHING IN THE DITCH** (page 41) of the seams between the blocks and along the borders. Then stitch diagonally through the blocks. Channel-quilt the borders and stitch around the outside, a scant ¼" (6 mm) from the edge.

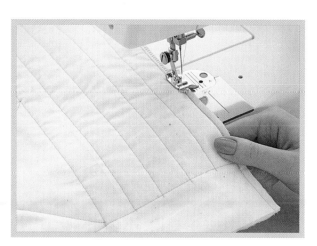

Perpendicular to the seam. If your triangle is symmetrical, your marked line should be 6" (15 cm) long. The height of the cover, from each end of the line to the bottom edge, should be 11" (28 cm).

17 Trim the batting and the backing even with the top layer on the long sides. Do not trim the short ends. Fold the quilted piece in half crosswise, aligning the border edges; pin. Stitch the sides, 1/4" (6 mm) from the edges. **FINISH** the seam allowances together, using a **ZIGZAG STITCH.**

18 At an upper corner, separate the front and back, forming a triangle, with the seam in the center. Mark a line 3" (7.5 cm) below the point, **perpendicular to the seam.** Pin along the line through all the layers; stitch, removing the pins as you sew. Trim off the point 1/4" (6 mm) from the seam, and finish the seam allowances together. Repeat for the opposite side.

19 Bind the lower edge, following the general directions on page 42, steps 5 to 9. In step 5, fold back the beginning end of the binding 1/2" (1.3 cm) and overlap the other end, forming a complete circle.

Bow Ties
Wall Hanging

The Bow Tie block has been a favorite of quilters for centuries because of its symmetry and clean geometric lines. The block is made using a simplified method of quick cutting and **CHAINSTITCHING.** Begin your fabric selection with a multicolored print for the borders and binding. Drawing colors from this print, select four small coordinating prints, or a combination of prints and solids. The wall hanging shown here is made from sixteen blocks of each bow tie color. Its finished size is about 37" (94 cm) square.

WHAT YOU'LL LEARN

How to choose several coordinating fabrics

A new way to piece triangles

The importance of accuracy in both cutting and piecing

How to arrange quilt blocks for interesting visual effects

WHAT YOU'LL NEED

⅜ yd. (0.35 m) each of four fabrics, A, B, C, and D, for bow ties

¾ yd. (0.7 m) background fabric

¾ yd. (0.6 m) fabric, for border and binding

1¼ yd. (1.15 m) muslin, for backing, plus 6" (15 cm), for hanging sleeve

Low-loft batting, about 41" (104 cm) square

ROTARY CUTTER AND MAT

Quilting ruler

Thread that matches one of your fabrics or harmonizes with all of them

Sealed wooden lattice, for hanging the quilt

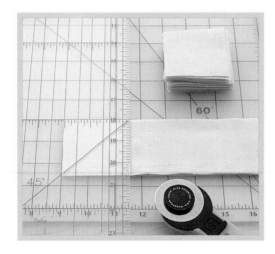

Let's Begin

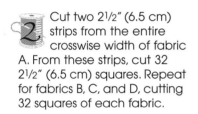

1 Straighten the cut ends of the fabric, and trim off the **SELVAGES** (page 31). Cut eight 2½" (6.5 cm) strips from the entire crosswise width of the background fabric. From these strips, cut 128 2½" (6.5 cm) squares.

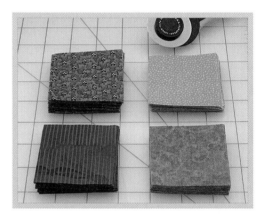

2 Cut two 2½" (6.5 cm) strips from the entire crosswise width of fabric A. From these strips, cut 32 2½" (6.5 cm) squares. Repeat for fabrics B, C, and D, cutting 32 squares of each fabric.

3 Cut two 1½" (3.8 cm) strips from the entire crosswise width of fabric A. From these strips, cut 32 1½" (3.8 cm) squares. Repeat for fabrics B, C, and D, cutting 32 squares of each fabric.

4 Cut eight 3" (7.5 cm) strips from the entire crosswise width of the border/binding fabric: four for the border, and four for the binding.

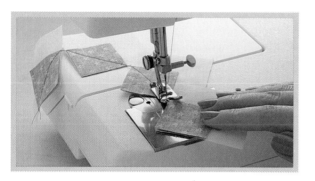

Chainstitching saves time and thread when piecing, because seams are sewn without stopping or breaking the stitching between pieces. When you get to the end of a seam, don't remove the fabric. Lift the presser foot, and position the next square in front of the needle. Then lower the presser foot, and continue sewing.

5 Place a 1½" (3.8 cm) square in one corner of a background square, with right sides together and raw edges even. With the stitch length set at 10 to 12 stitches per inch, which equals 2.5 mm, stitch diagonally from corner to corner of the smaller square. Without cutting the thread or removing the first pieced square from the sewing machine bed, repeat this step with a second set of squares. Continue in this manner until you have sewn all 128 sets of squares. This technique is called **chainstitching.**

6 Lay out the chain of squares on the pressing surface. **PRESS** all the small squares in half along the stitched lines, matching the outer edges to the large square.

7 Flip the squares over. Trim the large square and one layer of the small square at the stitched corner, leaving ¼" (6 mm) **SEAM ALLOWANCE.** Carefully clip all of the pieced squares apart.

8 With right sides together and raw edges aligned, join a pieced square to a large square of the same bow tie fabric, as shown. Stitch a ¼" (6 mm) seam. Use the chainstitching technique to join all the pieced squares in the same manner.

continued

continued

9 Lay out the chain of joined sets on the pressing surface. Press all the seam allowances toward the whole squares. Carefully clip all the sets apart.

10 Place two similar sets right sides together, aligning the seams at the center. The seam allowances will be pressed in opposite directions. ***Insert a pin in the well of the seams (p. 57),*** to make sure they line up exactly. Stitch a ¹⁄₄" (6 mm) seam, forming a Bow Tie block; remove the pin when you come to it. Use the chain-stitching technique to join all the sets into Bow Tie blocks.

TIP: For the first few sets, you may feel more comfortable pinning them together at the center seam. Once you get the rhythm, try stitching them together without the pin. Stitch slowly to ensure that the seams line up perfectly and the seam allowances stay pressed in opposite directions.

11 Lay out the chain of Bow Tie blocks on the pressing surface. Press all the seam allowances in the same direction. Carefully clip all the blocks apart.

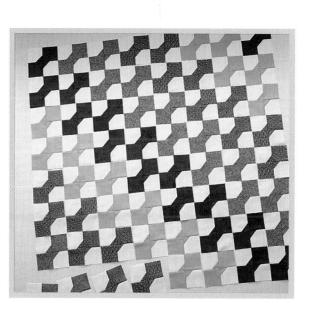

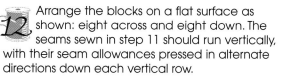
Arrange the blocks on a flat surface as shown: eight across and eight down. The seams sewn in step 11 should run vertically, with their seam allowances pressed in alternate directions down each vertical row.

Join the blocks in one vertical row, stitching 1/4" (6 mm) seams and beginning at the top. You should notice that all the aligning seam allowances are pressed in opposite directions. Press all the new seam allowances in the same direction. Replace the row on the flat surface.

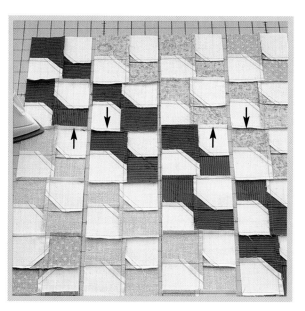

Repeat step 13 for each vertical row, pressing the seam allowances of adjoining rows in opposite directions.

97

continued

continued

15 Pin the rows right sides together, aligning raw edges and seams. Again you will notice that all the aligning seam allowances are pressed in opposite directions. Stitch a 1/4" (6 mm) seam, removing pins when you come to them.

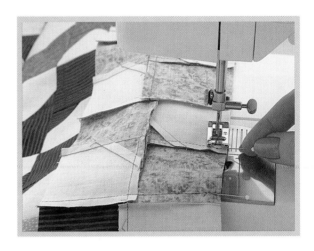

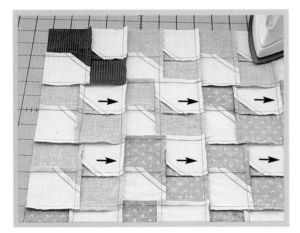

16 Press all the new seam allowances in the same direction. Lightly press the entire quilt top, first from the wrong side, then from the right side.

TIP: Now take a little breather. Stand back and admire your work. If you have sewn accurately, all your seams align, forming perfect intersections. That is quite an accomplishment!

17 Measure the quilt top across the middle. Cut two of the border strips equal to this measurement. Pin one strip to the top of the quilt; pin the other strip to the bottom. Align the ends of the strips to the outer edges of the quilt top. Stretch the strips or the quilt slightly, if necessary, to make them fit. Stitch 1/4" (6 mm) seams; press the seam allowances toward the borders.

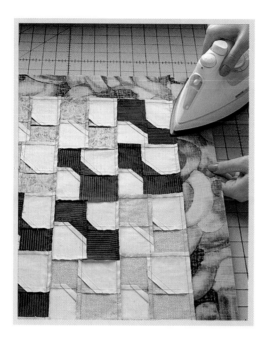

18 Measure the quilt top down the middle. Cut the remaining border strips equal to this measurement. Pin a strip to each side of the quilt, aligning the ends of the strips to the edges of the quilt top. Stretch the strips or the quilt slightly, if necessary, to make them fit. Stitch 1/4" (6 mm) seams; press the seam allowances toward the borders.

19 Cut the backing fabric and batting 4" (10 cm) longer and wider than the quilt top. Layer and baste the quilt (page 34). Attach a walking foot (page 9). Quilt by **STITCHING IN THE DITCH** (page 41), *following this sequence (p. 65).* Begin with the center vertical seam; then the center horizontal seam. Then stitch in the ditch of the seam between the border and quilt top. Finish by stitching the remaining vertical seams between block rows and the remaining horizontal seams between block rows.

continued

continued

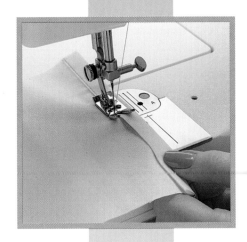

20 Bind the quilt, following the directions on page 42. Cut a piece of washed, unbleached muslin 6" (15 cm) long and the width of the quilt. Fold the short edges under 1/2" (1.3 cm) twice, and stitch a **DOUBLE-FOLD HEM** near the inner folded edge.

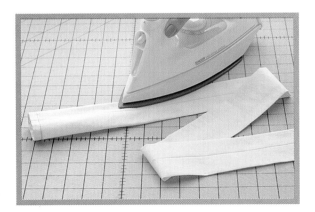

21 Fold the strip in half lengthwise, with right sides together and raw edges aligned. Stitch a 1/2" (1.3 cm) seam and press the seam allowances open. Turn the sleeve right side out; press it flat with the seam centered.

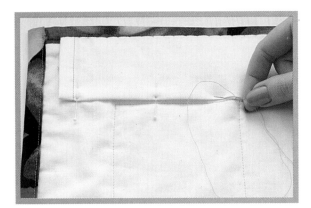

22 Pin the sleeve to the back of the quilt, close to the top edge and 1" (2.5 cm) from the sides. Slipstitch (page 58, step 14) the sleeve to the quilt along the upper and lower edges. Be sure to stitch through the backing and into the batting, but without stitching through to the quilt top.

23 Insert a strip of sealed or painted wooden lattice, cut 1/2" (1.3 cm) shorter than the width of the quilt, through the sleeve. Secure the lattice to the wall by sliding the quilt aside and inserting nails or screws 1/2" (1.3 cm) from the ends of the lattice.

Bow Tie
OPTIONS

Bow Ties is a versatile quilt design that lends itself to several block arrangements. Now that you've mastered the traditional pattern, try one or all of these alternatives:

Zigzag pattern has the quilt blocks turned in alternate directions.

Octagonal pattern is created by arranging the quilt blocks in units of four.

Staggered pattern of quilt blocks forms diagonal rows. This arrangement requires half-block sets at the top and the bottom of every other row.

Ohio Star Flange Pillow

Triangles are frequently used in quilt blocks. This pattern, called the Ohio Star, is made from both squares and triangles, and requires only three different fabrics. The quilt block itself measures 12" (30.5 cm), perfect for a small pillow. The border around the block becomes the pillow flange. The pillow back, sewn from the same fabric as the border, features a lapped closure, for easy insertion and removal of the pillow form.

Select a multicolor print for the center square, the border flange, and the pillow back. Draw colors from the print, in either solid colors or small prints, to repeat in the star points and the background pieces that complete the block.

WHAT YOU'LL LEARN

How to cut triangles

How to **CHAINSTITCH** triangles

How to make a flange pillow

How to sew a lapped closure

WHAT YOU'LL NEED

1 yd. (0.95 m) fabric A, for the center square, border flange, and pillow back

3/8 yd. (0.35 m) each of two fabrics, for the star points and background

1/2 yd. (0.5 m) muslin, for backing

4" (10 cm) of 3/4" (2 cm) hook and loop tape, for the closure

Low-loft batting, about 22" (56 cm) square

ROTARY CUTTER AND MAT

Quilting ruler

12" (30.5 cm) square pillow form

Thread to match or blend with the fabrics

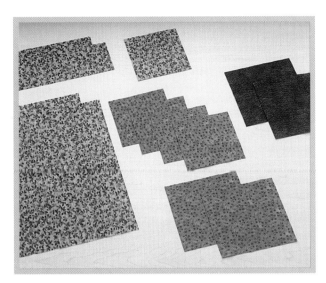

Let's Begin

1 Straighten the cut ends of the fabric, and trim off the **SELVAGES** (page 31). Cut two 3" (7.5 cm) strips from the entire crosswise width of fabric A for the border flange strips. Also cut two 12" x 19" (30.5 x 48.5 cm) rectangles for the pillow backs and one 4½" (11.5 cm) square from fabric A. Cut four 4½" (11.5 cm) squares and two 5½" (14 cm) squares from the background fabric. Cut two 5½" (14 cm) squares from the star point fabric.

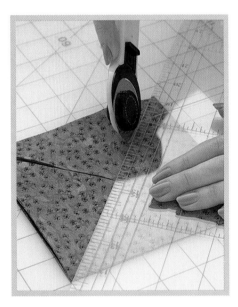

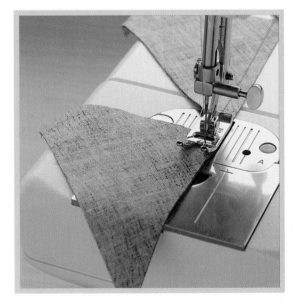

2 Layer the two larger background squares and the two star point squares, matching the raw edges. Cut through the squares diagonally in both directions, cutting them into triangles.

3 Align one star point triangle with one background triangle, right sides together. Stitch along one short side, taking care not to stretch the **BIAS** edges. Repeat for the remaining seven sets of triangles, chainstitching one right after the other, without cutting the thread. Place the fabrics in each set in the same position, and stitch the same edges.

Do not press them. At this point, pressing would distort the shape of the pieces, because they have been stitched on the bias.

4 Clip the sets apart. **Do not press them.** Place two sets right sides together, alternating fabrics. With your fingers, press the **SEAM ALLOWANCES** toward the darker fabric. Pin the pieces together along the long edge, *inserting the pins in the well of the seam (p. 57).*

5 Stitch the long **SEAM,** taking care not to stretch the bias edges and keeping the seam allowances turned in the direction they were **FINGER-PRESSED.**

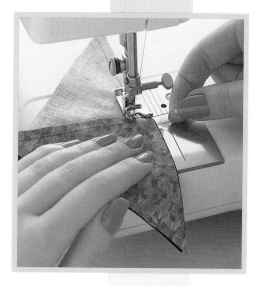

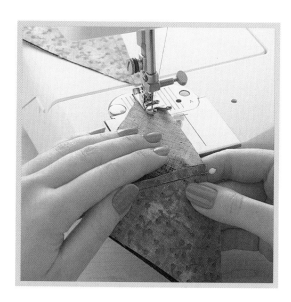

6 Repeat steps 4 and 5 for the remaining three sets, chainstitching one right after the other, without cutting the thread. Place the fabrics in each set in the same position, and stitch the same edges.

continued

continued

7 Clip the sets apart. **PRESS** the seams to one side. Trim off the points at the corners even with the sides.

8 Arrange the squares on a flat surface in the order shown. Stitch each horizontal row together. Press the seam allowances in the two outer rows away from the center square; press the seam allowances in the center row toward the center square.

9 Pin the vertical rows together, inserting the pins in the wells of the seams. Stitch the rows together, keeping the seam allowances turned in the direction they were pressed. Press the new seam allowances toward the center.

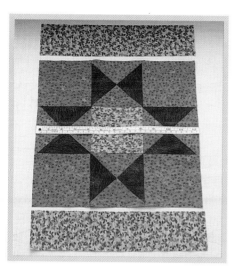

10 Measure the block across the center. Cut two border strips equal to this measurement. Pin one strip to the top of the block; pin the other strip to the bottom. Align the ends of the strips to the sides of the block. Stretch the strips or the block slightly, if necessary, to make them fit. Stitch 1/4" (6 mm) seams; press the seam allowances toward the borders.

11 Measure the block in the opposite direction across the center, including the new borders. Cut two remaining border strips equal to this measurement. Pin a strip to each side of the block, aligning the ends of the strips to the top and bottom edges of the block. Stretch the strips or the block slightly, if necessary, to make them fit. Stitch 1/4" (6 mm) seams; press the seam allowances toward the borders.

12 Cut muslin backing and the batting 4" (10 cm) larger than the pillow top. Layer and baste the pillow top as on page 34. Attach a walking foot (page 9). Quilt the pillow top, **STITCHING IN THE DITCH** (page 41) of the seam around the center square. Then stitch four diagonal lines through the triangle-pieced squares, beginning and ending at the border seam for each line. Stitch a scant 1/4" (6 mm) from the outer edge of the border. Trim the batting and backing even with the top layer.

continued

continued

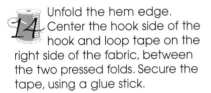 Press under 2" (5 cm) along one long edge of a back rectangle. Unfold the pressed edge. Turn the cut edge back, aligning it to the first foldline; press the outer fold.

Unfold the hem edge. Center the hook side of the hook and loop tape on the right side of the fabric, between the two pressed folds. Secure the tape, using a glue stick.

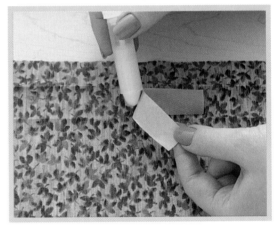

Edgestitch around the hook tape. At the corners, stop with the needle down in the fabric, and **PIVOT.** Overlap the stitches about 1/2" (1.3 cm) where they meet.

Edgestitch. Stitch as close as possible to the edge of the tape. Align the presser foot so that the needle will enter the tape just inside the outer edge. Determine the point on the presser foot that aligns to the outer edge of the tape. As you sew, rather than watching the needle, watch the edge of the tape pass under that point on the presser foot. Stitch slowly for best control.

16 Refold the hem along the pressed foldlines, encasing the raw edge, to form a 1″ (2.5 cm) **DOUBLE-FOLD HEM.** Pin the hem, inserting the pins perpendicular to the folds.

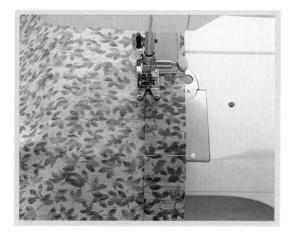

17 Place the pinned hem under the presser foot of the machine, with the wrong side of the pillow back facing up and the needle aligned to enter the fabric just inside the inner fold. Stitch along the fold.

18 Follow step 13 for the second pillow back piece. Pin the folded hem in place. Then follow step 17. Center the loop side of the hook and loop tape on the right side of the hemmed piece, between the fold and the stitching line. Secure the tape, using a glue stick.

continued

continued

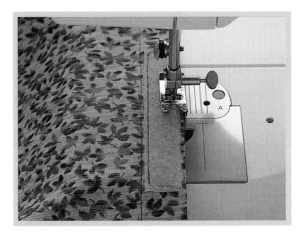

19 Edgestitch around the loop tape, pivoting at the corners and overlapping the stitches about 1/2" (1.3 cm) where they meet.

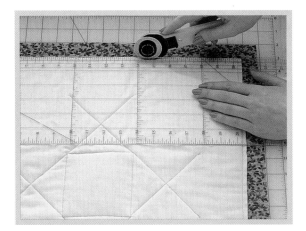

20 Overlap the two pillow back pieces, so that the foldline of the upper piece aligns to the stitching line of the lower piece. Seal the hook and loop tape. Trim the pillow back to the same size as the pillow front. Pin the raw edges together on each side where the hems overlap.

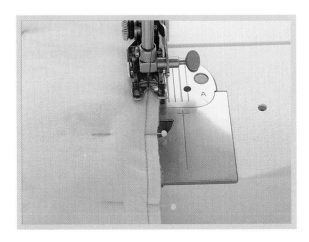

21 Pin the pillow front to the pillow back, right sides together. Attach a walking foot (page 9). Stitch completely around the four sides *1/4" (6 mm) from the edges.* Overlap the stitches about 1/2" (1.3 cm) where they meet. Trim the seam allowances diagonally at the four corners to remove excess bulk.

¹/₄" (6 mm) from the edges. In step 12, you stitched a scant ¹/₄" (6 mm) from the edges. Stitch just to the left of that first stitching line now, so that your first stitching line won't show on the outside of the pillow.

22 Turn the pillow cover right side out. Use a point turner or similar tool to carefully push the corners out, if necessary. Press lightly. Pin the layers together along the border seam, inserting the pins perpendicular to the sides.

23 Stitch in the ditch of the border seam, creating the pillow flange. Remove pins as you come to them. Stop stitching with the needle down in the fabric, to pivot at the corners. Overlap the stitches ¹/₂" (1.3 cm) where they meet. Now simply insert the pillow form and close the opening!

Flannel
Lap Quilt

Create a little coziness for cool evenings with this flannel lap quilt. Begin your fabric selection with a multicolor medium-size print flannel for the **SASHING** and borders. Then, for the **STRIP-PIECED** sections, select six flannels in colors to coordinate with the print. Pick fabrics of various **COLOR VALUES**, some in solid colors and others in small prints. You will also need a flannel fabric for the backing. The easy choice would be to repeat one of the strip-piecing fabrics. Ample fabric amounts are given below because flannel may tend to shrink more than other cotton. All **SEAM ALLOWANCES** are ¼" (6 mm). The finished lap quilt measures about 55" x 38½" (139.5 x 97.8 cm).

WHAT YOU'LL LEARN

How to strip-piece a quilt top

Flannel is easy to sew

WHAT YOU'LL NEED

1⅝ yd. (1.5 m) fabric, for the sashing and borders

⅝ yd. (0.6 m) each of six fabrics that coordinate with the sashing and borders

1⅞ yd. (1.75 m) fabric, for the backing (possibly repeat one of the other fabrics)

Low-loft batting, about 58" x 49" (147 x 125 cm)

ROTARY CUTTER AND MAT

Quilting ruler

Thread

Let's Begin

1 Straighten the cut ends of the fabric, and trim off the **SELVAGES** (page 31). Cut two 3" (7.5 cm) strips from the entire **CROSS-WISE GRAIN** of each of the six strip-piecing fabrics. Cut three 3½" x 45½" (9 x 116 cm) sashing strips *from the lengthwise grain* of the sashing/border fabric. Cut four 5½" (14 cm) border strips from the entire lengthwise grain of the sashing/border fabric.

2 Arrange six 3" (7.5 cm) strips in the order you would like to see them in your quilt. Place the first strip, right sides together, over the second strip, aligning the long edges. Stitch the strips together. Then stitch the third strip to the other side of the second strip. Continue adding strips in sequence until you have sewn the complete six-strip unit.

TIP: You can sew these strips together without pinning first, if you take your time. Keep the edges aligned and hold both strips with even tension. The strips may not be exactly the same length. Start with the ends evenly aligned and begin stitching from that same end with each additional strip.

3 Sew the remaining strips into an identical six-strip unit. **PRESS** all the seam allowances in the same direction. Cut the six-strip units crosswise into 5½" (14 cm) strips. You will need a total of twelve pieced strips. Discard any excess fabric.

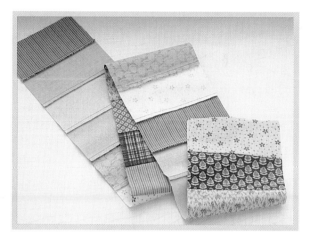

From the lengthwise grain. This eliminates the need to piece the sashing and border strips for the lap quilt.

Stitch three strips together, end to end, in the same sequence, to make one long eighteen-piece strip. Repeat until you have sewn four identical long strips. Press the new seam allowances in the same direction as the others.

Place one sashing strip and one pieced strip right sides together, matching the centers and ends. Pin along the length, easing in any excess fullness. Stitch the seam, removing pins as you come to them and keeping all the seam allowances turned in the same direction.

TIP: It is easiest to sew this seam if the pieced strip is on the bottom, with the seam allowances pressed toward you.

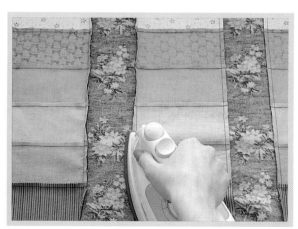

Stitch another pieced strip to the other side of the sashing. Continue until you have stitched all the pieced strips and sashing strips together. Press all the seam allowances toward the sashing strips.

continued

continued

7 Measure the quilt top across the middle. Cut two of the border strips equal to this measurement. Pin one strip to the top of the quilt; pin the other strip to the bottom. Align the ends of the strips to the outer edges of the quilt top. Stretch the strips or the quilt slightly, if necessary, to make them fit. Stitch ¼" (6 mm) seams; press the seam allowances toward the borders.

8 Measure the quilt top down the middle. Cut the remaining border strips equal to this measurement. Pin a strip to each side of the quilt, aligning the ends of the strips to the edges of the quilt top. Stretch the strips or the quilt slightly, if neces- sary, to make them fit. Stitch ¼" (6 mm) seams; press the seam allowances toward the borders.

9 Place the quilt top over the backing fabric, and trim the backing fabric to the same size. Layer both pieces, with the backing fabric on top, over the batting. Pin the layers together around the outer edge, using safety pins.

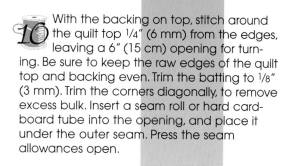 With the backing on top, stitch around the quilt top ¼" (6 mm) from the edges, leaving a 6" (15 cm) opening for turning. Be sure to keep the raw edges of the quilt top and backing even. Trim the batting to ⅛" (3 mm). Trim the corners diagonally, to remove excess bulk. Insert a seam roll or hard cardboard tube into the opening, and place it under the outer seam. Press the seam allowances open.

Turn the quilt right side out through the opening. Press lightly around the outer edges. Slipstitch (page 58, step 14) the opening closed, alternating small stitches from one side of the opening to the other.

Smooth the quilt out on a flat surface. Baste with safety pins, securing all three layers. Attach a walking foot. Quilt the lap quilt by **STITCHING IN THE DITCH** (page 41) of the border seam. Then stitch in the ditch of the seams between the sashing and the pieced strips, beginning with the center rows and working outward. Once you remove the safety pins, you're ready to cuddle up on the sofa with your new lap quilt!

Rail Fence
Wall Hanging

Rectangles can be found in dozens of block quilt designs. Here they're combined in the Rail Fence pattern to create a dynamic wall hanging. A light to dark progression of four fabrics accentuates the quilt's zigzag pattern. Select four small prints with **COLOR VALUES** that progress from dark to light. Or select two solids and two prints that give the same effect. A two-color border, using the two darkest fabrics, creates the illusion of a mat and frame.

All of the **SEAM ALLOWANCES** for this project are 1/4" (6 mm). Sew as accurately as possible to ensure perfectly matched **SEAMS.** The finished size is about 38½" x 30½" (97.8 x 77.3 cm).

WHAT YOU'LL LEARN

STRIP-PIECING
techniques

How to sew a quilt
with a
double border

How color arrange-
ment creates
optical illusions

WHAT YOU'LL NEED

3/8 yd. (0.35 m) fabric A
(very light)

3/8 yd. (0.35 m)
fabric B (light)

1/2 yd. (0.5 m)
fabric C (medium)

1⅝ yd. (1.5 m)
fabric D (dark)

6" x 30" (15 x 76 cm)
piece of muslin,
for hanging sleeve

Batting, about 42" x 32"
(107 x 81.5 cm)

**ROTARY CUTTER
AND MAT**

Quilting ruler

Thread

Let's Begin

1 Straighten the cut ends of the fabric, and trim off the **SELVAGES** (page 31). Cut six 1¹/₂" (3.8 cm) strips from the entire crosswise width of each of the four fabrics. Arrange the strips in four stacks (A to D) according to their color value, from lightest to darkest.

2 Pin an A strip and a B strip right sides together, aligning the long edges; insert the pins perpendicular to the long edge. Stitch the strips together, removing the pins as you come to them. Then stitch a C strip to the other side of the B strip, in the same manner. Add a D strip to the other side of the C strip. You should now have a pieced set, 4¹/₂" (11.5 cm) wide.

3 Repeat step 2 until you have six sets of pieced strips. **PRESS** all the seam allowances toward the darkest strips. Cut the strips, perpendicular to the seams, into 4¹/₂" (11.5 cm) squares. You should be able to cut at least nine squares from each set; you will need a total of 48 squares to make the wall hanging.

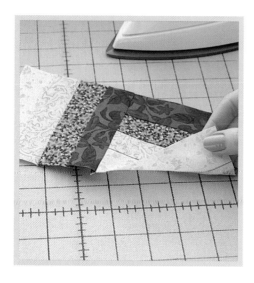

4 Stitch two squares, right sides together, in vertical-horizontal arrangement, with the darkest strips at the right and top. Press the seam allowances toward the vertical dark strip.

5 Stitch two more squares, right sides together, in horizontal-vertical arrangement, with the darkest strips at the top and right. Press the seam allowances toward the vertical light strip.

TIP: Be sure to keep the fabrics in the same sequence from left to right and top to bottom throughout the quilt.

6 Stitch the two sets, right sides together and seams aligned. ***Insert a pin in the well of the seams (p. 57),*** to make sure they line up exactly. Stitch them together, removing the pins as you come to them and keeping the seam allowances turned in the opposite directions. Press the seam allowance toward the lower set.

continued

continued

7 Repeat steps 4 to 6 until you have assembled twelve identical blocks. Arrange them in four rows of three blocks, on a flat surface. Stitch each horizontal row of blocks together, matching the seams and keeping the seam allowances turned in the direction they were pressed. Press the seams allowances in the top and third rows toward one side; press the seam allowances in the second and fourth rows in the opposite direction (note arrows). Return them to the flat surface.

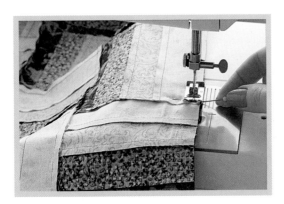

8 Place the top two rows right sides together, aligning seams. Insert pins in the wells of the seams, to make sure they line up exactly. Stitch them together, removing the pins as you come to them and keeping the seam allowances turned in opposite directions. Press the seam allowances toward the lower row. Continue until you have stitched all four rows together.

TIP: Press the quilt top lightly from the right side and then return it to the flat surface. Now, stand back and let your eyes play for a while over the nifty zigzag pattern you have created.

9 Cut four 1½" (3.8 cm) strips from the entire crosswise width of fabric C, for the inner border. Measure the quilt top across the middle. Cut two of the border strips equal to this measurement. Pin one strip to the top of the quilt; pin the other strip to the bottom. Align the ends of the strips to the outer edges of the quilt top. Stretch the strips or the quilt slightly, if necessary, to make them fit. Stitch ¼" (6 mm) seams; press the seam allowances toward the borders.

10 Measure the quilt top down the middle. Cut the remaining border strips equal to this measurement. Pin a strip to each side of the quilt, aligning the ends of the strips to the edges of the quilt top. Stretch the strips or the quilt slightly, if necessary, to make them fit. Stitch 1/4" (6 mm) seams; press the seam allowances toward the borders.

11 Cut four 2½" (6.5 cm) strips from the entire crosswise width of fabric D, for the outer border. Measure for and apply the outer borders in the same manner as the inner borders.

12 Cut the backing fabric and batting 4" (10 cm) longer and wider than the quilt top. Layer and baste the quilt (page 34). Attach a walking foot (page 9). Quilt by **STITCHING IN THE DITCH** (page 41), *following this sequence (p. 65).* Begin with a diagonal path near the center, stitching along both sides of the darkest zigzagging strip. Then stitch around both border seams. Finish quilting the remaining zigzagging strips. Bind the quilt (page 42). Add a sleeve for hanging, following steps 20 to 23 on page 100.

Glossary

APPLIQUÉ. This French word refers to a decoration or cutout that is applied to the surface of a larger piece of fabric. Many methods of appliqué are used, including simply machine stitching around the outline of the decoration or hand stitching invisibly.

BIAS refers to the diagonal direction of a piece of fabric. True bias is at a 45-degree angle to both the lengthwise and crosswise grains. Woven fabric has the greatest amount of stretch on the bias.

CHAINSTITCHING. Sewing several individual seams without breaking the stitching threads between the pieces, thus saving time and trips to the ironing board.

COLOR VALUE. The relative lightness or darkness of a color. In selecting fabrics for a quilting project, it is often necessary to judge the value of various fabrics, both solid colors and prints.

CROSSWISE GRAIN. On woven fabric, the crosswise grain runs perpendicular to the selvages. Fabric has slight "give" in the crosswise grain.

DOUBLE-FOLD HEM. Hems that are made with two folds of equal depths, encasing the cut edge in the crease of the outer fold.

FAT QUARTERS. A half yard (0.5 m) of fabric, cut down the middle to measure 18" x 22"

(46 x 56 cm). This is the equivalent of a quarter yard (0.25 m) of fabric.

FINGER-PRESS. Rather than use an iron, temporarily press seam allowances to one side with the fingers. This is usually done on bias seams to avoid distortion.

FINISH. To improve the durability of a seam, the raw edge is secured with zigzag stitches that prevent raveling. This is important whenever narrow seam allowances are exposed and must withstand repeated handling or laundering.

GRAINLINE. Woven fabrics have two grainlines. The lengthwise grainline runs parallel to the selvages. It is the strongest direction of the fabric with the least amount of "give." The crosswise grainline runs perpendicular to the selvages and will "give" slightly when pulled.

LENGTHWISE GRAIN. On woven fabric, the lengthwise grain runs parallel to the selvages. It is the strongest direction of the fabric with the least amount of "give."

LOFT refers to the thickness and springiness of the batting.

PIVOT. Perfect corners are stitched by stopping with the needle down in the fabric at the exact corner, before turning the fabric. To be sure the corner stitch locks, turn the handwheel until the needle goes all the way down and just begins to rise.

PRESSING. This step is extremely important to the success of your quilting projects. Select the heat setting appropriate for your fabric, and use steam. Lift and lower the iron in an overlapping pattern. Do not slide the iron down the seam, since this can cause the fabric to stretch out of shape, especially on the crosswise grain or bias.

ROTARY CUTTER AND MAT. This timesaving method of cutting fabric may take a little practice and serious precautions. The blade on a rotary cutter is extremely sharp. Cut slowly, watch your fingers, and <u>always</u> retract or cover the blade between cuts. The rotary cutter cannot be used without the special cutting mat.

SASHING. Strips of fabric, plain or pieced, that are sewn between the square block units of a quilt.

SEAM. Two pieces of fabric are placed right sides together and joined along the edge with stitches. After stitching, the raw edges are hidden on the inside, leaving a clean, smooth line on the outside.

SEAM ALLOWANCE. Excess fabric that lies between the stitching line and the raw edge. Stitching with a narrow 1/4" (6 mm) seam allowance is traditional for quilting projects because it minimizes the bulk of fabric behind narrow strips and points.

SELVAGE. Characteristic of woven fabrics, this narrow, tightly woven outer edge should be cut away. Avoid the temptation to use it as one edge of a quilting piece, since it may cause seams to pucker and it may shrink excessively when washed.

STITCHING IN THE DITCH. An easy and often-used quilting technique that gives definition to blocks, borders, and sashing. Place the quilt under the presser foot so that the needle stitches between two fabrics and into the well of the seam.

STRIP PIECING. Creating pieced designs from long strips of fabric by stitching the strips together lengthwise and then cutting them crosswise. This method saves time over cutting pieces individually and then sewing them together.

TENSION. When your machine puts the same amount of "pull" on both the top thread and the bobbin thread, your stitches lock exactly halfway between the top and bottom of the fabric layers. Even tension is essential for successful sewing. Some sewing machines require minor tension adjustments when switching from one fabric to another.

ZIGZAG STITCH. In this setting, the needle alternately moves from left to right with each stitch. You can alter the width of the needle swing as well as the length of the stitch. A zigzag stitch that is twice as wide as it is long gives you a balanced stitch, appropriate for finishing the edge of a seam.

Index

A

Accessories, sewing
  machine, 8-9
Adjusting tension, 15
Appliqué, 124
Appliqué hot pad,
  raw-edge, 47-51

B

Backing fabrics, 25
Backstitch, 37
Balancing tension, 14-15
Basic quilting techniques,
  38-41
Basting, 34, 36-37
Batting, selecting, 29
Bias, 23,124
Binding, 42-45
Bobbins, 9
  winding, 11
Bow Ties wall hanging,
  93-101

C

Chainstitching, 124
Channel quilting, 41
Checkerboard placemats,
  61-65, 67
Color value, 124
Cover, sewing machine, Log
  Cabin design, 85-91
Crosswise grain, 23, 124
Cutting mats, 18-19
Cutting tools, 18-19

D

Definitions, 124-125
Double-fold hem, 124
Double nine-patch table
  topper, 69-75

E

Embroidery presser foot, 9
Equipment,
  see: Supplies
Eraser, fabric, 19

F

Fabric, 23-25
  selecting, 26-27
Fabric eraser, 19
Fat quarters, 77, 124
Feet, presser, 9
Finger-press, 124
Finish, 124
Flange pillow, Ohio Star
  design, 103-111
Flannel lap quilt, 113-117

G

General-purpose presser
  foot, 9
Glossary, 124-125
Grainline, 124
  crosswise, 23, 124
  lengthwise, 23, 124

H

Hand quilting, 38, 39
Hem, double-fold, 124
Hot pad, raw-edge
  appliqué, 47-51

I

Ironing,
  see: Pressing

J

Jam, thread, 17

L

Lap quilt, flannel, 113-117
Layering, 34-36
Lengthwise grain, 23, 124
Loft, 124
Log Cabin sewing machine
  cover, 85-91

M

Machine quilting, 38, 40-41
Machine, sewing,
  see: sewing machine
Marking tools, 19
Mats, cutting, 18-19
Measuring tools, 18-19

N

Napkins, 66
Needles, 20
  sewing machine, 8, 10,
Nine-patch pillow, 53-59

O

Ohio Star flange pillow,
  103-111
Outline quilting, 41

P

Parts of a sewing
  machine, 7
Pencils, 19
Pieced sashing table runner,
  77-83
Pillows,
  nine-patch design, 53-59
  Ohio Star flange, 103-111
Pins, 20
Pivot, 124
Placemats, checkerboard
  design, 61-65, 67
Preparing fabric, 25
Presser feet, 9
Pressing (ironing), 57, 124
  equipment and tech-
  niques, 21
Print fabrics, 24
Projects,
  Bow Ties wall hanging,
    93-101
  checkerboard placemats,
    61-65, 67
  double nine-patch table
    topper, 69-75
  flannel lap quilt, 113-117
  Log Cabin sewing
    machine cover, 85-91
  napkins, 66
  nine-patch pillow, 53-59
  Ohio Star flange pillow,
    103-111
  pieced sashing table runner,
    77-83
  Rail Fence wall hanging,
    119-123
  raw-edge appliqué hot
    pad, 47-51

Q

Quilting techniques, basic,
  38-41
Quilt, lap, flannel, 113-117

R

Rail Fence wall hanging,
  119-123
Raw-edge appliqué hot
  pad, 47-51
Rectangles, rotary cutting,
  32
Rotary cutters, 18, 125
Rotary cutting, 30-33
Ruler, 19
Runner, table, pieced
  sashing, 77-83

S

Safety pins, basting with, 37
Sashing, 125
Scissors, 19
Seam, 16-17, 125
Seam allowance, 125
Selecting,
  batting, 29
  fabrics, 26-27
Selvages, 23, 125
Sewing machine, 6
  accessories, 8-9
  inserting the needle, 10
  Log Cabin cover, 85-91
  parts, 7
  threading, 12
  winding the bobbin, 11
Shears, 19
Solid fabrics, 25
Special-purpose presser
  foot, 9
Squares, rotary cutting, 32
Stitches,
  backstitch, 37
  chainstitch, 124
  stitch-in-the-ditch, 41, 125
  zigzag, 125
Stitch-in-the-ditch quilting,
  41, 125
Strip piecing, 125
Strips, rotary cutting, 32
Supplies,
  marking tools, 19
  measuring and cutting
    tools, 18-19
  pins, needles and
    thread, 20
  pressing equipment, 21

T

Table runner, pieced
  sashing, 77-83
Table topper, double
  nine-patch design, 69-75
Techniques.
  basic quilting, 38-41
  pressing (ironing), 21
Tension, 125
  how to balance, 14-15
Terms, 124-125
Testing tension, 14
Thread, 20
  basting with, 36
Threading the sewing
  machine, 12
Thread jams, 17
Tools, 18-19
Topper, table, double nine-
  patch design, 69-75
Triangles, rotary cutting, 33

W

Walking presser foot, 9
Wall hangings,
  Bow Ties design, 93-101
  Rail Fence design, 119-123
Winding the bobbin, 11

Z

Zigzag stitch, 125
Zipper presser foot, 9

CREATIVE PUBLISHING international

President: Iain Macfarlane
Group Director, Book Development: Zoe Graul
Director, Creative Development: Lisa Rosenthal
Executive Managing Editor: Elaine Perry

Project Manager: Jill Anderson
Senior Editor: Linda Neubauer
Art Director: Mark Jacobson
Assisting Art Directors: Eileen Bovard,
  Delores Swanson
Copy Editor: Janice Cauley
Researcher: Janice Rapacz
Writers: Amy Boxrud, Linda Neubauer
Lead Project Stylist: Wendy Fedie
Project & Prop Stylists: Coralie Sathre,
  Joanne Wawra
Sample Production Manager:
  Elizabeth Reichow
Lead Samplemaker: Carol Pilot
Sewing Staff: Diana Colardi, Diane Combites,
  Arlene Dohrman, Sheila Duffy, Sharon Eklund,
  Phyllis Galbraith, Teresa Henn, Muriel Lynch,
  Virginia Mateen, Delores Minkema,
  Nancy Sundeen, Joan Wigginton
Senior Technical Photo Stylist: Bridget Haugh
Technical Photo Stylists: Sharon Eklund,
  Kathleen Smith, Nancy Sundeen
Studio Services Manager: Marcia Chambers
Photo Services Coordinator: Carol Osterhus
Senior Photographer: Chuck Nields
Photographers: Rex Irmen, Andrea Rugg
Senior Photography Assistant: Greg Wallace
Scene Shop Carpenter: Dan Widerski
Manager, Production Services: Kim Gerber
Production Manager: Patt Sizer
Mac Designers: Laurie Kristensen, Jon Simpson,
  Brad Webster
Production Staff: Curt Ellering, Laura Hokkanen,
  Kay Wethern
Contributors: Coats & Clark Inc.; Fairfield
  Processing Corporation; Hobbs Bonded
Fiber; Olfa® Products International;
Spaceboard™, Volster Marketing

Printed on American paper by:
R. R. Donnelley & Sons Co.
10 9 8 7 6 5 4 3

Creative Publishing international, Inc.
  offers a variety of how-to books. For
  information write:
      Creative Publishing international, Inc.
      Subscriber Books
      5900 Green Oak Drive
      Minnetonka, MN 55343

*Due to differing conditions, materials, and skill
levels, the publisher and various manufacturers
disclaim any liability for unsatisfactory results or
injury due to improper use of tools, materials,
or information in this publication.*